Three W's

Tears of Pain and Joy

Ernest Gaines

This book is a work of non-fiction. Unless otherwise noted, the author
and the publisher make no explicit guarantees as to the accuracy of
the information contained in this book and in some cases, names of
people and places have been altered to protect their privacy.

Archway Publishing books may be ordered through booksellers or by contacting:

Archway Publishing
1663 Liberty Drive
Bloomington, IN 47403
www.archwaypublishing.com
1 (888) 242-5904

Because of the dynamic nature of the Internet, any web addresses or
links contained in this book may have changed since publication and
may no longer be valid. The views expressed in this work are solely those
of the author and do not necessarily reflect the views of the publisher,
and the publisher hereby disclaims any responsibility for them.

Any people depicted in stock imagery provided by Getty Images are
models, and such images are being used for illustrative purposes only.
Certain stock imagery © Getty Images.

Scripture quotations are from the ESV® Bible (The Holy Bible, English
Standard Version®), copyright © 2001 by Crossway, a publishing ministry
of Good News Publishers. Used by permission. All rights reserved.

ISBN: 978-1-4808-7940-9 (sc)
ISBN: 978-1-4808-7941-6 (e)

Library of Congress Control Number: 2019907698

Print information available on the last page.

Archway Publishing rev. date: 6/24/2019

About the Author

Ernest Gaines is a six generation Share Cropper born March 10, 1954, in Oscar, Louisiana. Ernest moved to California in 1969 where he met his wife of 42 years (Lorraine), they have four children, 10 grandchildren, and 3 great grandchildren. Ernest is retired from Napa Valley College.

He gave his life to Christ and has worked faithfully in the ministry ever since July 3, 1998. Ernest received his Certification of Ordination as a Deacon in 1998 from Liberty Missionary Baptist Church Vallejo, California and had worked in the ministry ever since.

Ernest was called to the office of ministry to become a license Minister January 17, 2016, from Church of The Living God Vallejo, California and he continues to work in His Kingdom at Hillside Church Gulfport, Mississippi under the leadership of Dr. Travis Anderson; and lead people to Christ.

God has called me to be a faithful worker and be committed to His Word.

Inspiration and Acknowledgements

To all the men's and women's before and with me from the Quarters that didn't quit.

Also

Thanks to my Grandparents, Uncles, and Aunts that gave me the opportunity to come to California and see the world through a different set of lenses.

Dedicated

To My Angel Lorraine the Love of My Life who became my wife who has been by my side for 48 years, who has made all this possible at age 17 when I wanted to end it all she said no, I will not let you quit.

Preface

3 W'S Tears of Pain and Joy

Keep in mind this story is about a boy from March 10, 1954 – September 1969. Somethings I witness or went through and others I was told of incidents that happened which made me ask questions. Even today at the age of 65 years old I still have no answers. The tears I shed was real and the pain it caused never seemed to go away. But, in time it made the heart stronger, the skin thicker, and his walk-in life couldn't be stopped. Each moment of my life even if it was painful it made me stronger and determine not to stop or quit. I never said no to anything that I was asked to do, even if I felt it was not right or if it had a purpose. I held nothing against him. I didn't get mad, I was a child and was told you're supposed to do what your parents ask of you.

As, I look back over my life I would tell him thanks, you made me a stronger man, even to the point that you never let your beginning determine your ending and let no man or no one tell you what you can and can't do. I was told that I was not worth nothing and will never become nothing. What he didn't know as a young boy I hated to lose, that's why I never quit or stopped learning to work hard and set goals. I wasn't going to let him win.

I want you to ask yourself after reading my story if this sound like you, or your life what choice did you make? Remember failure comes from quitting, and quitting was a choice I was determined not to give up or give in to negativity. There is a saying that what don't kill you will make you stronger, don't become a failure because someone tell you that you will. Whatever choice that you choose, keep in mind that's the choice you made so don't blame someone else.

Contents

Chapter 1

Family

They called me Plook. I was born in Oscar, Louisiana, on March 10, 1954. My mother's name was Vean, my father's name was Gabby, and my grandfather's name was T-Moon, and my grandmother's name was Lena.

When I was older, I rode on T-Moon's shoulders from Lodio Plantation to Major Plantation and got into the wagon to ride into the woods with Par, as I called him. He would hitch two mules to the wagon. Sally was a big white mule with big eyes that was always flapping her tail, while Nelly was big and brown.

I was maybe four or five years old, so everything looked big to me. We would head into the woods, and along the way, people on the road or sitting on the porch, or garry as we called it, would wave at us.

In the woods, Par would chop down a tree, cut it up with a saw, and load the pieces into the wagon. He would pick and eat black fruit called muscadine. He gave me one; it was bitter, and I spat it out and wiped my mouth with my hand and shirt, and they would turn black. Par told me not use my shirt; he wiped my mouth with a rag he carried. Oh he would be mad, and Granma would fuss with him when we got home because my clothes would have stains on them.

We would head back to the Quarters. Some of the same people were still on their garrys waving at us. They would say, "Hi, Mr.

T-Moon," and he would say hi back to them. There was always something different; the kids would be playing in the yard running around trying to catch each other. Some would be hiding, and the older people would wave rags over themselves to keep the 'skeeters from biting them.

As I got a little older, I'd go to church across the road from where Par and Granma lived. I would play hide-and-seek with the kids. Someone would start counting while the rest of the kids would hide, and once they were spotted by the seeker, they had to run and beat the seeker back to the base.

We had very few if any toys, but we had so much fun running, hiding, and laughing with each other while the old people would be in the church talking about what I couldn't tell you. We were not to come in where grown-ups were talking, so we always played outside. They would give us sandwiches—peanut butter and jelly—Kool-Aid, watermelon, and popcorn balls.

Once I got older, we started playing different games—we'd shoot marbles, spin tops, and play peach stone and jacks. We would also play knuckle; if you lost, you got hit on the back of your hand. We had fun with simple things—sticks, brooms, or mop handles one of the older boys would cut for us to use as a bat, and we used rocks as baseballs. Oh boy, did I get in trouble when I cut down a broom to make a bat. My dad made me sweep the house with that very short broom.

The older boys had a rubber ball and a bigger stick they called a bat. There were many of us around my age who would play: Jamp, Topcy, and Hook were around my age. The older boys would hit the ball, and we kids would run after it and bring it back to them. We also played football. Someone would throw it, and the others would chase and tackle whoever caught it. Oh, that was fun.

As I got older, I don't know what happened, but Par didn't come and get me anymore from my house. I asked my mother why he hadn't come to get me, and she said he was sick. I guess I was seven or eight then. My father would take me to the Quarters, give me a sack, and tell me to pick cotton. He would fuss every day because I couldn't fill the sack.

I was no longer able to play with the other kids. It would be almost dark when I came home, and I had to feed the dogs, chickens, and hogs. He used to hunt, so I had to feed the dogs when he brought them back late from hunting in the woods, and sometimes, it would be very dark and the 'skeeters would be biting.

After school, I would come home and start my chores all over again—feeding the dogs, hogs, and chickens, watering the garden, picking whatever needed to be picked from it, and weeding it with a cane knife or hoe.

One Sunday, I went to church in the Quarters. I used to walk about half a mile with some older girls. Par and Granma lived across the road, and after church, I would walk to their house. One time, Par was sitting in a wheelchair with a blanket across his lap. I asked him where he had been, and he said he was sick. There was a ball on the floor, so I asked him to play with me. He would throw the ball to me, but I would miss it, and the ball would bounce all over the front room. Granma Lena would yell, "Stop before you break something!" so I asked Par to go in the yard and play with me. He started to cry and said he couldn't walk or stand up. I asked him why, but all he did was cry. Granma said he'd had a stroke. I didn't understand what that meant.

As I got older, maybe eight or nine, I saw very little of Par. I worked more in the fields with my father, and then Par died. I could no longer ride on his shoulders or ride in the wagon pulled by Sally and Nelly. I didn't play with the other kids anymore. I was always working in the fields or at home. My mother became sick, so I had to learn how to wash clothes in a tub using a washboard, hang them out to dry, and iron them. I learned how to cook butter, pinto, and red and white beans with sausage and rice.

I liked going to school. I would play with all the kids from the Quarters and Lodio at St. Alma's School. Oh what fun that was. The other kids would ask me to come and play with them after school.

We played in the field where there were no crops, cane, corn, or cotton. I could never finish playing because when my father got home, he would send for me and whip me because I hadn't done my chores. I did them, but I couldn't wait for morning to come so I could go to school and play with my friends.

My dad had an old baseball glove; he used to play first base. I thought he and I could play catch together, but he gave the glove to my older cousin. I would watch that cousin and his father and other kids and their fathers playing catch in the field. I had a lot of fun playing baseball and football when they let me play, but as soon as my father got home, he would send for me.

When I was about eight or nine, my uncle came from California; he bought me a rubber ball and glove, and we played catch. At the time, we were living on Lodio Plantation. Sometimes when I was by myself, I'd simply throw the ball up and catch it or throw it at the hen house or outhouse and catch the rebounds. I took my ball and glove to bed with me and to school in my book sack. One day, someone took my ball and glove out of my book sack, and I found out who had done that. Mr. George, the principal, made him give them back to me. I didn't like that boy at all.

As I got older, I played with the older boys at school and with Jamp, Topcy, and Hook, who were around my age. My father would play catch with the other kids but not with me.

The next time my uncle came from California, he and I played catch. He gave me a football; he'd tell me to run, and he would throw it to me.

One time, I asked him, "Where's California?"

"It's far away," he said.

I didn't know where that was, but I said, "Yes sir."

He came once or twice a year like my Grandma and Grandpa did as they lived in California also.

I want to thank the Father who loved me then and loves me now. My other father couldn't kill me because he didn't know I had a purpose and someone to love me.

I was told that when I was about six months old, he tossed me into a fig tree. I cried all night; he left me hanging there while he went to work. My head was stuck in the fork of the tree, and my legs were dangling. I cried as loud as I could. I was told that an angel climbed into the tree and got me out. I was taken to the hospital in New Orleans, where I stayed for months and was treated for spinal meningitis.

When I was about seven, my arm got caught in the wringer of a washing machine when I was playing with a sock pulling it in and out. Par was in a wheelchair; he and I were the only ones home, and he was able to get my arm out.

Chapter 2

My Brother

I was about eight or nine when I found out that Jamp and I were brothers. We got into a fight at school over who got to sit in Topcy's desk as he was absent that day. We were sent to Mr. George, the principal, who whipped us with his belt. We were sent back to class and had to sit in our assigned seats. Mr. George gave us notes to take home. I gave mine to my mother, who read it. She looked at me and smiled. She puffed on her cigarette and coughed as if she were clearing her throat. She said, "Boy, you tell him about this when he gets home."

About an hour or so later, I was feeding the hogs when he got home and got out of his truck. I said, "Hi."

He looked at me and asked, "Have you fed the chickens and my dogs?"

"Yes sir."

"You have some tomatoes that need to be picked."

"Yes sir, I'll pick them."

I went in about twenty minutes later with the tomatoes. "Did you tell him who you had a fight with at school today?"

I didn't say anything. He looked at me with that look—I knew I was in trouble. I knew the next words out of his mouth would be, "Go get a switch." That's what they called them. I had to get the longest one I could find. I opened my mouth while he was still staring at me and about to pee on myself. I said, "Jamp."

He took a piece of chicken my mother had fried and said, "Boy, get in the truck."

He was silent as we drove. When we got to the Quarters, he tossed his chicken bone out the window. Some people had started to move out of the Quarters. My grandfather had died, and my granma lived where we lived, on Lodio Plantation. I wondered where we were going. I knew Jamp still lived down in the Quarters. My dad drove down to the end of the road. I wondered if he was looking for a big switch to whip my butt with. He stopped at Jamp's house. His mother was sitting on the garry smoking. My dad rolled down his window and asked her, "Where is that boy at?"

"In the house," she said.

"Tell him to come here."

She turned and said, "Jamp, come here."

When Jamp came to the door, my father said, "Boy, come here."

He and I got out of the truck as Jamp came over. His mother was still just smoking on the garry. I balled my fists as tight as I could. I was ready. I was sure he was going to make us fight each other because they did that all the time on both plantations. He would always say, "You're not going to be a coward," but that time, he said, "Let me tell you two little boys something. Y'all are brothers. I don't never again want to hear that y'all been fighting each other, y'all hear me?"

"Yes sir," we said. We looked at each other and hugged. He opened the door to get back into the truck. I didn't ask him anything as we drove back home, and he didn't say a word. Boy was I glad he didn't whip me.

When we got home, my mother was still sitting there smoking. She didn't say anything, but she didn't look mad.

I said, "He's my friend, and if he's my brother, why don't he live with us?" All my other brothers and sisters lived together.

The next day at school, we told Topcy and Hook that we were brothers, but no one believed us, and not even the adults could tell us how that had happened. *How's that possible?* I wondered. *He lives in one place and I live somewhere else. Who am I? Where did I come from? Am I supposed to be here?*

But Jamp and I played with each other as usual; nothing changed. I was living on Lodio Plantation and he was living in Cherie Quarters, but we went to St. Alma's together.

Chapter 3

An Angel with Me

I was around nine or ten when one day while I was planting sugar cane, the bib, the hook of the cane knife, got stuck in the top of my foot. When I pulled it out, a piece of meat about two or three inches long came out with it. He took a knife out of his pocket, cut it off, and threw it away. He put some mud on my foot and tore his shirt so he could bandage it up. He said, "Get back to work."

Thank God for being there and looking over me. He said, "I will never leave you or forsake you." I knew that whenever something didn't go as planned but I was still around and able to talk about it, it was because I had an angel with me.

We moved from Lodio Plantation to Frisco, and I started going to school in New Roads. I played baseball, basketball, and football and ran track; after school, I would stay and play with the kids. One of my teachers who lived close to me would give me a ride home after I played with my friends after school. We used to choose teams, and I would always get picked. There were always people cheering for the other kids, my friends, but no one for me that I knew of. As I got older, I was told things that made me ask a lot of questions, but I received no answers from him or her. *Who am I? Where am I going? What am I doing here? But I'm not alone! Why doesn't anyone love me? Never give up! God be with me!* I've never seen the Father who loved me. He held me tight. I can't help myself. They gave up on me. As I get into my story as I was told, I learned there was a God who loved and was always there.

But even with an angel in the fields with me, I didn't know who I was or was supposed to be, what to look for or even hope for. I looked around the fields and even behind the wagon and tractor, but I saw no one my age. Where were the guys I shot marbles with, played with tops, yo-yos, baseball, or hide-and-seek—Jamp, Topcy, and Hook? When I worked in the fields, none of my friends were there.

Frisco was an area without many houses. Next to our house was a cow pasture with rabbits, chickens, other birds, snakes, and deer. I would walk to the back of the yard where there was some water and trees. I used to watch him go back there to kill ducks and sometimes catch fish he said we couldn't eat.

One day when he was working, I took his gun, went to the back of the yard, and shot a bird. Oh man, did that scare me. Pulling the trigger knocked me on the ground and hurt my arm and shoulder. I left the bird, picked up the gun, and ran back to the house. I knew I was in trouble. I thought I had done something wrong with his gun because he never was knocked over by it. I put the gun next to the bed where he always kept it. I knew I was in trouble. She was in the kitchen when I came back. She asked me where I had been. I told her the backyard. She said, "Don't you go back there in the woods. I heard someone shooting back there. Go to the hen house and bring me two eggs."

"Yes ma'am."

I got the eggs for her. She was standing by the back door and yelled, "Catch that chicken!"

I ran after the chicken and caught it next to the fence. She said, "Wring its neck." I had never done that before, but I had seen her and others do that, and I wanted to. I spun the chicken around by its neck, but the head didn't come off. She told me I had to keep turning it around and around until the head came off. I tried it again, but again, the chicken would just fall to the ground and hop around. I had blood on my hands, but the chicken still had its head.

"Boy, bring me that chicken." She was standing on the back porch with a knife in one hand and a cigarette in the other. "Put it there on the step over yonder and move back." She put the cigarette in her mouth, held the chicken with one hand, whacked its his head off with the knife, and kicked the chicken to the ground. She tried to throw the head on top of the hen house but missed. She said, "Boy, go and throw that head on top of the hen house."

"Yes ma'am."

The chicken flapped its wings and hopped all over the backyard for maybe thirty minutes. She went back inside, and later, she said, "Boy, bring it here."

I brought the chicken to the kitchen. She told me to put it in the sink. She poured hot water on it. She told me to wait about ten minutes and start pulling the feathers off. I started to pull the feathers; some would come off easily but others were hard to pull. I plucked and plucked until she told me, "Okay, that's good enough. Have you done the rest of your chores?"

"Yes ma'am."

"Have you fed the cows, hogs, chickens, and dogs?"

I said, "I'll do that right now."

"Okay," she said. "I don't want to hear that man's mouth today."

Even after all that, I still didn't know who I was and who I was supposed to be. I was ten or eleven then, and I wanted to be with my brother Jamp and my friends Topcy and Hook at Lodio Plantation—not Frisco.

Chapter 4

Picking Peas

It was summer—time to pull corn and pick up hay off the ground and put it on the back of the wagon. One morning, he woke me up about six and told me to get dressed. "You're going to work," he said.

I put on some blue jeans that were too big and long for me. I had no belt, so he gave me a piece of rope they used to bale hay, and I tied together the two loops on either side of my jeans. I put on a white T-shirt and some work boots he gave me. He drank some coffee, and I had a glass of milk. He said, "Let's go."

We got into the truck and rode about a mile to a house. A little white man came out and asked me, "Boy, how're you doing?"

"Okay sir," I said.

He said, "This is Mr. Jarran."

I shook his hand. He had a tractor running with a wagon hooked up to it. He told me to get on. I hopped up on the wagon. He got in his truck and drove off. Mr. Jarran turned the wagon around, and we started down the field. He stopped and gave me a straw bushel basket. He asked, "Have you picked peas before?"

"No sir."

"I'll show you how to pick them, and I'll give you twenty-five cents for each bushel you pick."

I started to pick the peas up and down the rows on my knees. It took me about an hour and a half to fill the bushel basket. I said, "Mr. Jarran, I have a bushel full."

"Okay, boy. Put it on the back of the wagon and get another one."

"Yes sir."

At noon, he asked me, "What did you bring for dinner?"

"Nothing, sir."

"How long did you think you was going to work?"

"I don't know sir. He didn't tell me."

"Here." He gave me a slice of bread with a slice of pepper sausage. "Eat this, but tomorrow, bring your dinner."

"Yes sir."

We sat under a pecan tree and ate. He took his knife out of his pocket and sliced up an onion. He put some on some bread and drank a jar of water. I sat there watching him; he closed his eyes for about five minutes. He swatted at a fly that landed on his forehead and said, "Okay, boy, it's time to go back to work."

I filled up six bushels, and he said, "You earned a dollar and a half, but I'll pay you two dollars because you worked hard today. I'll see you tomorrow. Is your pa coming to get you?"

"He did not say so, sir."

But I could walk home, so I did. I did the same thing all summer.

Chapter 5

School

A man who drove a school bus lived across the street from our house. He told me he would be taking my sister and me to school. He told us to be ready at 6:30 in the morning. I was happy to be going to school.

Mr. B, the driver, was a big, yellow man. The first day, he turned on False River Road, which was not the way to St. Alma's. He stopped in front of a school, and I started looking around for Jamp, Topcy, and Hook but didn't see them. Come to find out, they were going to a school the other way close to St. Alma's and I was going to Rosenwald, ten miles away. I began to ask myself again, *Who am I? Am I supposed to be here? Where am I going?*

I was twelve then. I started making friends and playing baseball, basketball, and football and running track. Once again, I saw parents cheering for their kids but no one cheering for me or calling me son, holding my hand, giving me support, and taking me home. *What am I doing here? Is this where I'm supposed to be?*

I took the bus home or got a ride from one of my teachers. *Where's my brother Jamp I used to play with?* I made friends; we played a lot together, and I was having fun, but something wasn't right.

I got up in the morning depending on the time, season, or weather. If it was cold outside, I had to start a fire in the fireplace to heat up the house before anyone got up, even him. He didn't get up until the house was warm. My mother would fix breakfast and help get my sister and brothers ready for school, but some mornings, she couldn't get up because she was sick a lot. She had asthma, and she smoked and coughed a lot. He used to fuss at her about smoking, and sometimes when she left her cigarette in the ash tray, he would throw it outside, but that didn't stop her from smoking. She would sit down at the table in a chair or on the sofa and roll another one. Yep, she would roll her own cigarette like most people did then. One tobacco she used a lot was in a red package called Target. If she didn't feel like getting up to light it, she would say, "Boy, come here."

I had three brothers in the house, but I knew she was calling me, so I would say, "Yes ma'am" or "I'm coming." I would take her cigarette to the kitchen or the fireplace, whichever was closer, and try to light it. Most of the time, the cigarette would be out by the time I got it back to her, so she would make me try again and again. She'd be coughing so hard that I didn't think she'd stop. "Boy," she'd say, "You're going to buy me some more 'bacco. Ya wastin' my money burning my cigarettes up. I told you to draw on it to keep it lit or put it in your mouth and puff on it."

I tried that, but it would make me cough, and my eyes would water up. Then she would get mad and get up and light it herself. "You better hurry up. The bus will be here any minute, and you better be ready. When you cut Ms. Clurok's yard, you're going to buy me some mo' 'bacco." I guess I was supposed to answer her because she'd ask, "Boy, you hear me talkin' to you? I ain't playing with you no!"

"Okay, yes ma'am."

"Ain't that Mr. B blowing his horn for y'all? Y'all better get out of here and go catch that bus fo' he leaves you."

We would run to the bus. I always liked to sit by a window so I could look for my brother and friends from the Quarters I used to play with at the church house and on the merry-go-round at St. Alma's. We used to play baseball and football on the big field. I tried to spot my friends but couldn't because of the big trees. I used to say that one day, I'd walk through the trees because I knew they were on the other side.

When we got to False River, Mr. B would always turn left, and I needed to go to the right—yep, that's where my brother and friends were. I wondered if they were looking for me. I'd look for them in all the passing cars but never saw them. On our way to school, I'd see the sign pointing to the left that said New Roads and the sign pointing to the right that said Lakeland, the way to the Quarters, Lodio, and St. Alma's School because Lakeland was where we used to live on Lodio Plantation after we moved from Cherrie Quarters, where I met my brother Jamp and my friends.

We used to see each other at school every day and on Sunday. Many times, I would walk to church with some older girls because he wouldn't let my mother drive there and she couldn't walk that far. It was about a mile or more. I was the oldest, so she would let me walk by myself, but my sister and brothers were too young. She would walk with me to the road, and when she saw the girls going to church, she would wave. I was about eight or nine then, and the girls would always tell me how cute I was. At church, I would see all my friends, my Par, and Granma Lena.

After church, I would play with my friends and cousins and eat at their house until the older girls would say, "Okay, let's go, Plook." That's what they called me. I would hug Granma and Par, and we would head back to Lodio. The girls would walk me around the curve to where the road would get straight, and they would watch me go home. I would be so happy because I had played with my brother and friends and had seen Par and Granma. Yep, we had moved out of the Quarters, but we still saw each other every day at school and at church.

But after we moved to Frisco, I couldn't see my brother and friends anymore. I knew that Par had died, and Granma was living on Lodio with my aunt and her kids. But I knew where my friends were. I just had to find a way to get past those trees and see Jamp. I still didn't know why we weren't living together. If we had been, we could have played every day as we used to.

Chapter 6

Looking for Jamp

One day, I asked my mother why my brother didn't live with us, but she didn't tell me. She just kept smoking and looking at me with a half-smile. She said, "Boy, go play." I never stopped looking for him and my other friends. I wanted to know why Jamp didn't live with us, and I wanted to find out. We don't know why or how we became brothers. Yep, I had a sister and brothers, but I saw them every day. It wasn't the same.

One day, I thought I had found out how to get to the Quarters behind them trees. I walked into our big backyard, where he used to hunt and fish. As many times as I had been back there, I had never seen my friends or my brother. After riding the bus again, I noticed that Lakeland was toward the Quarters and St. Alma's was the same way. I walked into the woods, but I must not have walked far enough because I saw no one. There were no peas to pick, and no school. My mother was in the house with my sister and brothers, and he was at work. I went into the bedroom and got his gun and started walking toward those trees again.

I got to the lake. To get to the other side, I had to walk to the left of the big yard next to the fence where I had shot a blackbird the previous week. I was walking with the gun on my shoulder the way he would. I walked along the fence for about thirty minutes and saw no one. I heard only birds. I heard a woodpecker, but I never saw it.

I kept on walking. The grass and bushes were getting taller and thicker. I had been walking for an hour, and I was getting tired and hungry. I came to a barbwire fence and crawled through it. I walked maybe another ten or fifteen minutes. I heard some cows mooing, and I saw a big pasture through the trees. Yep, I was tired and started to get scared, but I wasn't going to stop until I had found my brother and friends.

I walked past a gravel road with a ditch full of water next to it. I saw a black man on a tractor who was stirring up a lot of dust. He saw me and stopped. He wiped his face and the inside of his hat with a white handkerchief. "Boy, who are you? What are you doing out here? What are you hunting? Who are your kinfolks What's your name?"

"Plook," I said.

"Who's your pa?"

"Gabby."

"Where do you live?"

"Frisco. I'm going to Cherrie Quarters to visit my brother and my friends."

"Who's your brother, boy?"

"Jamp, sir."

"Where's Cherrie Quarters?"

"Major Plantation."

"Well, it's over yonder, but you're not going to get to it this way. The way you're going is the wrong way. If the man who own this land catches you around his cows with that gun, he'll shoot you."

My knees stared shaking. "I'm sorry, sir. Can you tell me how to get out of here and get to the Quarters?"

"Where did you say you came from?"

"Frisco."

"Frisco?"

"Yes sir." I began to get even more scared.

"How did you get here?"

"I walked through them trees over there."

"How long have you been walking? You must have been walking a long time, but you're going the wrong way. You said Cherrie Quarters?"

"Yes sir."

"You're about five or seven miles from there or maybe farther. You're headed toward Livonia. You gotta be tired, boy. To get to the Quarters, you have to go through False River. To get to Cherrie, you need to go back the way you came, but you better not go that way. You could get in trouble because that old man doesn't like people on his property if he doesn't know their folks."

He looked at me and wiped his forehead and the inside of his hat again. He spit something brown. I figured he was chewing 'bacca.

"Hand me that gun," he said.

I handed it to him. He stuck his hand out. "Give me your hand." I did, and he pulled me up onto the tractor. He said, "Stand right here. I'll take you over that way, the way you came. Go home before you get into trouble."

He took me to that barbwire fence. "This is as far as I can take you," he said as he gave me my gun.

"Thank you sir."

I started to walk back the way I had come. I started to cry after about thirty minutes of walking through the woods and trees. The grass looked like it had gotten taller. I kept walking, but I didn't know where I was going—nothing looked the same. I'd walk a little bit and then run, but it looked like I was going the wrong way to get home.

After about an hour and a half, I saw some trailers and a pink house. I began to really cry. I was so scared because I didn't recognize anything, but I kept walking. I saw a man on a horse, and I said, "Sir, I'm trying to get home."

"Where you from, boy?"

"Frisco."

"Well, that's where you are."

I looked around but didn't recognize anything. "Sir, which way to my house?"

"Where do you live?"

"In a grey house, sir."

"Keep walking straight where that pink house is, and get on the road out there boy, and go right."

I went to the road and started walking to the right. After walking for about ten minutes, I saw the house and field where I had picked peas. I began to see and know where I was going. He had never taken us anywhere. Where I had picked peas was the farthest I had ever been from home before then. I only knew the way the bus would take us to False River.

The old man rode up on his horse and yelled, "You're not far. Keep walking, boy." He rode off.

About ten minutes later, I saw my house. I ran home. My mother asked, "Where you been?"

"In the woods hunting, but I didn't kill nothing."

I put his gun back in the bedroom and went out to sit on the back porch.

It had been about two or three years since I'd seen my brother and my friends. I was thirteen. I still didn't know why Jamp didn't live with us. I thought it was like what had happened to my brother she had given to her sister, TT, who didn't live with us either. Yep, I tried to figure it all out as I stared into those trees, but I had no answers. I started to think that someone may have given me to them because there was something different; it seemed no one had loved me but Par, and he had died. Yep, once again I was sitting in the backyard on the garry looking toward those trees where I knew he was. *Who am I? What am I doing here? Where am I going?*

Chapter 7

School Starts

School was starting in a couple of days. *Yep, I'll see my new friends and play with them.* On the first day of school, I got up, dressed, and caught the bus. When we got to the end of the road at False River, the bus driver turned to the left. I looked to the right but saw no one.

At school, my math teacher was standing at the door saying good morning to everyone. For PE, my friends and I played football and went back to class until lunch. After lunch, we had more classes, and at the end of the day, I took the bus home and as usual fed the chickens, cows, hogs, and his dogs and picked peas and hay. One good thing I didn't have to do in Frisco was pick cotton, cut or plant sugar cane, and pull corn.

But he found another job for me and my brother to do. He gave me a lawn mower, cane knife, and yo-yo blade that we used to cut weeds or grass that was two tall to cut with the lawn mower. I started doing that when I was about thirteen and my brother was about nine or ten; he wasn't that much help. We had two yards we cut including Ms. Clurok's yard, which was big yard. She would give him $25 for us to cut her yard. On Saturdays, he drove us and the mower and tools to False River. Again, I would look to the right to where Jamp lived, but he would turn left like the bus driver did.

We used to cut Ms. Labo's yard; it was very big also. She had a house in the back and a store in the front. She had a very small front yard, but her backyard went all the way down to the river. It would take us up to three hours to cut her grass, but before we could get started on her grass, we would have to throw rocks at the gators to get them back in the river. Then we would have to pick up the rocks so they wouldn't break the blades.

She used to wait until he got there to give him the $40, but one day, she gave me the money. My brother and I were sitting on the garry in front of the store. I saw my brother pull a sweet roll from under his shirt and eat it as we were waiting on him to pick us up. I asked, "Boy, where did you get that from?"

My brother starting stuttering; I didn't understand what he was saying, but I knew what had happened. I went into the store and paid for the sweet roll hoping she hadn't seen him take it and was waiting to tell him when he came that my brother had stolen it. My brother and I were both hungry, so I told him to get a cold drink to go with his sweet roll. He got a pineapple soda, and I got a red cream soda and a honey bun. Everything was about 40¢. I knew I wasn't supposed to spend any of the money, but all I could think of was when we were living on Lodio Plantation when I was about eight or nine. My cousins and I used to go to Mr. Bee's store the store to buy items for our parents. On the counter were peanuts, chips, gum, and candy, and when Mr. Bee went to the back to get something, they would fill their pockets and we would go under the house and eat all they had taken.

One day, she sent me to buy some pepper sausage, and when Mr. Bee went to the back to get it as he always did, I stuffed my pockets with peanuts, gum, and life savers. When he came back, I paid him for the sausage. He said, "Thank you. Tell your pa I want to see him when he gets home."

I said, "Okay sir." I took the sausage home and put it on the kitchen table. I hurried back outside and went under the house with Lassie, my dog, a collie just like the one on TV. Our house was high off the ground; you could almost stand up under it. My cousin and I used to play there especially in the summer as it was cool under there.

I ate some of my candy, and I hid the gum on top of a brick. I heard him pull into the yard; he was home from work. I came from under the house, and he asked me if I had done my work. I told him I'd fed the chickens, hogs, and dogs. "Mr. Bee wants to see you at the store. He told me to tell you that when you came home."

"What does he want?"

"I don't know. He just told me to tell you to come by."

He gave me his black lunch bucket and started walking to the store, which was across the road. I went in and set his lunch bucket next to the sink. I went outside and saw him waiting for a car to pass by so he could cross the road. I ran underneath the house for a piece of gum and went to the yard.

He came back and said, "Come here, boy." I walked toward him. "What did you do at the store today?" I said I had bought some pepper sausage for Mama. "What else did you do?" he asked.

I said, "Nothing."

"Go inside and sit at the kitchen table."

He got a knife out of a drawer. "What did you did at the store?"

"Nothing, sir."

"Put your hand on the table." He put the point of the knife on my hand. "What did you do, boy?"

"Nothing."

He pressed a little harder on my hand with the knife. "What did you do?"

"Nothing, sir." I really couldn't think of anything I had done wrong; my cousins took candy all the time. I also knew Mr. Bee hadn't seen me take the candy, so I didn't know what he was trying to get me to say.

He asked me again, "What did you do?"

"Nothing, sir."

He pressed a little harder, and blood started coming out of the back of my hand. I shouted, "I took some candy from the store!"

He hit me with the back of his hand. "No one in this family is a thief. You ask for it or you work for it. I have never been to jail, and no one in this family will go to jail for stealing."

"Yes sir."

He gave me the knife and told me to go outside and cut him a switch. He wanted a big one. We used to call them doctor switches. They grew long, tall, and skinny. At my age then, eight or nine, they looked like trees.

I went out for a switch and gave it to him. He told me to take my shirt off and lean over the chair. He started to hit me across my back with the switch. It seemed that every time he hit me, I saw pieces of the switch fall to the floor. He said, "This switch is to damn small." He stabbed me with the piece he was holding, and I thought he was finished, but he said, "Don't move." He grabbed the extension cord the fan was plugged into and started whipping me with it. The cord was hurting so badly that I started to jump around. "Put your hand on the back of the chair and don't move!"

It seemed that every time he hit me, my back would burn, and it started feeling like it was wet. I was crying and saying that I was sorry, that I wouldn't do it again. He told me to shut up. "When I finish with you, I know damn well you won't do it again."

He kept on whipping me. I saw pieces of the cord flying everywhere. He told me to shut up. When he stopped, I looked around and saw drops of blood on the floor. He then beat me with a rubber track he took of my brother's toy bulldozer, and when that broke, he took off his belt and beat me with that. It didn't matter what I said about how sorry I was, he didn't stop whipping me.

He told me to stand there. He went outside, and I saw him holding the knife he had stuck my hand with. He came back in with a long piece of rubber from his truck. "Lean over that damn chair you little piece of trash!" He started to hit me across the back again, and my whole body went numb. I didn't cry. I saw blood on the wall, table, floor, and even on him.

She came into the kitchen and grabbed a big, black skillet. "That's enough! You're going to kill that boy!"

"I bet he won't steal again!" He hit me again.

She said, "If you hit him again, I'll bust you in the head with this skillet!"

He told me to go to my room. She told me to take my bath and go to bed.

I was hurting so badly that I don't remember much after that or the rest of the night. I don't remember if it was he or she who woke me up and told me to get ready for school. I went to the bathroom and tried taking my pajama top off, but it was stuck to my back. It was so painful that I started to cry. I tried to take it off slowly, but that hurt even more. I guess I had been taking too much time because sister and brother had to use the bathroom also and kept knocking on the door. I kept telling them to wait.

He came to the bathroom door. "Boy, what are you doing in there? Hurry up!"

I came out of the bathroom, and he asked, "Didn't you sleep in that shirt?"

"Yes sir."

"Take that damn shirt off!"

"I can't." I was crying.

"Why in the hell not?"

"It's stuck to my back."

"What in the hell do you mean it's stuck?" He snatched it up over my head. I started screaming it was hurting so badly. He told me to get back into the bathroom and lean over the sink. He poured a bottle of green alcohol on my back that made my back feel even worse. I couldn't stop crying. He left for work, and she came into the bedroom and told me to go back to bed; she said I didn't have to go to school that day. As I was lying in bed, I was crying and shaking.

That was on my mind when my brother stole that sweet roll. I didn't want him to do the same to my brother, so I spent some of the money Ms. Labo had given me. When he picked us up, he asked why I was short 40¢. I told him that we were hungry; he fussed all the way home and hit me upside my head. "Don't you ever do that again without asking."

When we got home, he took me to Ms. Clurok's house and made me pull weeds from her flower beds and told my brother Rick to go into the house. I asked myself, *Am I supposed to be here? Who am I and what did I do wrong?*

Chapter 8

Onions

She was always sick. As the oldest, I had many responsibilities including cooking as I mentioned. I cooked standing on a chair or a bucket so I could see inside the pot. Cooking was not bad, but cutting up onions was; that would make my eyes burn so badly that I couldn't see what I was doing.

She would always get up and taste what I was cooking and tell me to add water if it was too thick or if it needed salt or pepper. If it was too watery or the beans were too hard, she would tell me to cook it a little longer. The first time I just quartered the onions to keep my eyes from watering so much, she looked in the pot and asked, "Boy, why didn't you cut them onions up?"

"I did cut them up."

"That's not how you're supposed to cut them up."

Yep, she gave a big spoon and told me to get the onions out of there and cut them up properly, but they had cooked too long and were falling apart. They looked smaller, however, so I put them back into the pot, stirred them up, and let them continue to cook.

She came back, looked into the pot, and said, "Boy, you know that's not how that's supposed to be. You better do something before he gets home."

When he came home, he looked into the pot and said, "Boy, bring your butt here." I was sure I going to catch it. "What's this?" He showed me some onions he had scooped out of the pot with a spoon.

"Onions."

"Take them all out and cut them up the way you were supposed to." He hit me upside my head.

"Yes sir."

He hit me upside my head again. "You better not never do that again. You know better. Look at me when I'm talking to you! I'll tear your butt up next time."

I never cut onions just into quarters after that.

Chapter 9

Chores

One evening as I was walking out the back door, he asked, "Boy, have you done your work?"

"Yes sir."

"I just came from outside, and it don't look like them damn hogs or dogs have eaten yet."

"Yes sir, I fed them when I was outside about an hour ago."

"Boy, that was too damn early. Go out there and feed them again or they'll be out there hungry all night. The hogs too. If they get out of the pen looking for food in the middle of the night, you're going to get your butt up and catch them."

"Okay sir."

I had many things to do, but at least when there was no school, I didn't have to comb my two sisters' hair. When he would go to work, I would ask her if I could go fishing or hunting with this old man, Mr. Budo. He was tall and skinny, and he liked to hunt rabbits. Smoky, his dog, was a little brown and black beagle that would chase rabbits from their nests or under bushes, and we would take turns shooting them. I wasn't a bad shot at age thirteen, and I shot one almost every time it was my turn. Mr. Budo would say, "Pretty good shot, young buck." We fished for catfish, buffalo, and carp in the lake back in the pasture and cleaned them at his house.

We didn't have the best clothes or places to live, but we always had plenty to eat. He kept the freezer full of meat you name it—deer, rabbits, raccoons, hogs, cow, fish, chicken, and all types of vegetables including mustard and collard greens; string, butter, and pinto beans; tomatoes; cucumbers; squash; pumpkins; watermelons; sweet potatoes; and potatoes. You name it, he had it.

My grandmother and grandfather came from California it seemed every year, and they would bring us boxes of clothes. They were always too big, but he would tell me I had to wear them. We had to roll up pants legs and sleeves. The coat sleeves were long enough to cover my hands, so I had to roll those up too. He'd stuff socks, rags, or paper into my shoes so they would fit.

He knew when my grandparents were coming; he would tell us not to mess with certain things in the freezer or in the kitchen. He would set aside frozen raccoon, rabbit, deer, hog, and fish and all types of vegetables for them to take back. He would help his parents load a big box on top of their station wagon when they went home to California.

Chapter 10

Hunting

Yep, one thing for sure—he loved to fish and hunt, and they said he could swim like a fish. He had never taken me fishing on False River, where he went all the time, but my Granma Lena, TT, and Dave took me fishing all the time.

One Friday night, he was cleaning his gun because he was going hunting in the morning, and he noticed that some of his bullets and shotgun shells were missing. He woke me up and asked me, "Who told you to mess with my stuff?" When I didn't say anything, he said, "Boy, don't you hear me? I'm talking to you."

"Yes sir."

"You're going to buy me some more bullets, you hear?"

"Yes sir."

He walked out of the room still fussing.

When I cut the grass at Ms. Clurok's on Friday, he kept the money and had me wash her car and sweep her garry and walkway. I don't know how much extra she gave him, but he kept it to pay for his bullets.

About two weeks later, he asked, "Boy, do you want to go hunting with me?"

"Yes sir."

He woke me up the next morning at five, but it was still dark, and I tried to get back to sleep. He told me to start a fire; he wanted a house already warm when he got up. It was real cold outside that morning, and because there wasn't enough wood in the house, I had to get some from the back porch, which was white with ice. As I was starting the fire, he yelled, "How's the weather?"

"It looks like it snowed."

"That's frost, boy."

I had no idea what that was.

He gave me rubber boots to put on that were too big, and a thick, plaid shirt that was also too big. He gave me some brown gloves, a sweater, a hat, and a green rain coat. He put some bread and pepper sausage into his black lunch bucket and poured coffee into a thermos. He gave me those, and he carried the guns. "Let's go, boy." We got into the truck, drove to the spillway, and pulled up next to some trees. About three or four white guys were talking next to their truck; they had been waiting for us.

He gave me the 30.06. He and the others discussed where each would be, and he told me to follow him. I followed him into the water, which was maybe a foot deep, but it was cold. He told me stand right there until he came for me. "No matter what happens, you better not move or you might get shot, you hear me?"

"Yes sir."

"Don't you move. Watch out for them snakes and the 'gators."

I started to get scared. "What do I do if I see one?"

"Don't move and don't make no noise. You'll scare the deer away."

I thought I should never have come, but I didn't want to tell him that; he would have given me a whipping. Every time something moved or made a noise, I got more scared.

About an hour and a half later, I couldn't see him, but I heard his voice very low saying, "Look to your right." I guessed he wasn't far away. I couldn't see him; I guessed he saw me, but I didn't know if he was talking to me or not. He said a little louder, "Boy, look to your right. Don't move or say anything. Just listen. Do you see it?"

I looked to my right and saw a big deer with a huge set of horns. I got scared all over again. The deer had its head in the air as if it were looking for something. I had never seen a live deer before; it looked like a little horse. "Do you still see it, boy? Don't say nothing. Raise your gun. Look straight down the barrel. Shoot it right underneath its back or front legs."

I was scared. My heart was pounding. My hands were all sweaty. He said, "When you see it in your sights, pull the trigger." I looked down the barrel. The deer was just standing there. I saw its front legs and stomach. I pulled the trigger, and the deer jumped. I thought I had missed it.

Then there he suddenly was standing next to me. "You hit it." One of the other hunters was pointing and saying, "It fell over yonder."

I didn't know what to do because he had told me not to move no matter what. But he said, "Boy, come on." They were laughing. One hunter was standing over the deer holding it by the horns and said, "Look what you got, boy. That's one good shot."

He and the others each grabbed a leg and lifted the deer out of the water. Its tongue was hanging out of its mouth. They carried it to the truck. He cut the deer's neck, and they put it in the back of the truck. They stayed for a while laughing and talking. He told me to get into the truck. When we got home, he told me to take the guns inside.

He came in after me and told her, "The boy shot a deer." He went back outside, and Mr. Lejon, who lived across the street, asked, "What y'all got there?"

He said, "The boy shot an eight-point buck."

"How big?"

"Two hundred and eighteen pounds. I left him at Mojo's to clean and cut up for us."

That was my first and only deer. He never took me hunting again. I would still hunt with Mr. Budo. He did give me a twelve-gauge shotgun, which was a lot of fun even if it scared me to death when I shot it.

Chapter 11

Our New House

It was time again for school. I still hadn't seen Jamp or the others from the Quarters since we had moved. I had met him at St. Alma's. I was taller and skinnier than he was. We would say hi to each other at school and on Sundays back then.

He was different from my sisters or brothers I lived with. I had to watch over them at home, on the bus, and at school, but most of the time, they'd get mad at me and wouldn't listen. I think that was the difference between them and Jamp. Though there was that difference, I loved them and would protect them; I wouldn't let anything bad happen to them or let anyone mess with them. I'm sure I would have protected Jamp also. One of my brothers lived with TT and Dave, and he had everything he wanted, even a horse.

One day, I came home from fishing with Mr. Budo and learned one of my brothers had been hit by a truck. My oldest sister and the others were at the house; my father and mother were in New Roads at the hospital. They came home and said he would be all right but would have to stay in the hospital for a few days.

Come to find out, he was going across the street to Ms. Clurok's house and he was following after him. He had to be about three or four then. He walked out into the street and was hit by a lumber truck. They said he was lucky to be alive. I thanked God for protecting him.

I helped take care of him when he got out of the hospital. He had cuts on his forehead, arms, and side. I'd change all his bandages several times a day. He would cry a lot when it was time for his bandages to be changed; I had to hold him on my lap to get him calmed down. He had some broken or cracked ribs that were very painful, and it took a long time for him to heal.

I don't remember all the details, but he said we had to move. He had told the owner of the place that he wanted to raise more cows and hogs, and the owner told him he couldn't do that. I was told that the insurance company had given him some money; he bought a lot in New Roads, and he planned to build a house near the school I was going to, Rosenwald.

One day, he told the bus driver that I wouldn't be going home on the bus. After that, I would meet him at the lot after school, and we would cut trees and weeds until late. He'd leave his tools there under a tree, and after school the next day, I would go there and work. Most of the time, I would be on my knees with a hand saw trying to cut down trees as close as I could to the ground. When he got there, he would help me, and we'd go home at dark. He would bring some diesel fuel from the steel mill he worked at in Baker, and we'd burn the trees and weeds with that. I don't know how many snakes I killed. I don't know how many got away.

We worked at the lot for months. One day, I got there and saw that someone had poured the cement foundation. I dug up and chopped the roots of trees as best I could.

Shortly after that, I went there one day after school and saw framers building our house. Four or five months later, we moved in. I was fourteen then.

After we finished moving everything from the house in Frisco, I looked over at those woods and trees as always but didn't see Jamp and my friends. I thought he might have moved away.

Yep, he had a car, but we never rode in it. He would be in it by himself; even she didn't ride in the car with him. Again, I asked myself, *Who am I? What am I doing here? Where am I going?*

Chapter 12

School in New Roads

One good thing about moving to New Roads was that I didn't have to catch a bus to go to school because my school was just about in our backyard. Our school was first grade through sixth and ninth through twelfth grades. The school down the street about a block away was where one brother and sister attended seventh and eighth grades. I would walk them almost to their school, watch them go to their classes, and run to my school.

I was very smart; I made the honor roll every year. My situation outside of school was better than before; he was working at a steel mill, so I had no farm work to do—no more cotton, hay, or peas to pick any more. I had only a few things to do—cut the grass, and if she wasn't feeling well, make sure my sister's and brothers' hair was decent and make sure they had lotion on their faces, arms, and legs.

You know how kids like to play on the way to school. We would walk out the backyard onto the track and football field; our house was between the twenty- and forty-yard lines. My sisters liked to race each other. I'd yell at them, but their legs and socks would be all dusty. I would try to wipe the dust off, but the more I wiped, the dirtier they got. She would yell at me every evening to make sure my sisters stayed out of the dirt, but the next morning, they would do the same thing.

I didn't walk home with them in the evenings because I was playing sports—football, baseball, and track. I was happy we had moved to New Roads because I didn't have to catch a bus, so I could play with my new friends more. It was almost like it used to be when I was playing with Jamp and my friends in the Quarters and at St. Alma's. At St. Alma's, we just picked teams and played, but at my new school, coaches chose the teams and gave the players different colored shirts.

My football coach asked me what positions I had played before, and I told him I ran with the ball. The first few times I did, I messed up because I wasn't used to playing with a helmet with that face guard. I took my helmet off, and he asked me why. He put my helmet back on my head and moved it around; he asked me who had given it to me. I told him Mr. Jones. He told me that my helmet was too big and had the wrong type of face guard. He gave me another helmet, and it fit better; the face guard no longer blocked my vision.

One time, the quarterback called a play and gave me the ball. I started to run but was tackled. The coach yelled that that wasn't what I was supposed to do. He had a playbook with a diagram that showed me where I was supposed to go. "Now you run right there!" I said, "Yes sir." I got the ball again and made about fifteen yards before I was tackled—much better.

The more I practiced the plays, the better I became, and I even made a touchdown one game. My teammates were hugging me, and we were all happy and laughing. As I got to the sidelines, however, I didn't see him or her.

The coach switched me to defense, and on my first play, three of my teammates and I tackled the runner, number 30. That was fun. That was how we played in the Quarters and St. Alma's.

I scored three touchdowns against the McKinley School team, but no one in my family saw that. After showers and changing clothes, my friends would wave goodbye to me as I walked across the field to my home. At home, I would say hi to my sisters and brothers, who would be watching TV and he and she would be lying in the bed with the door open. I would say hi to them. He would say nothing, but she would say, "Your food is on the stove." I'd start in on my homework because I wasn't hungry; they fed us after each game.

I was playing with the freshman team; we played six games, and the next four, I played on the junior varsity team. There were about a dozen of us whom the coach let play on that team. We had some good-looking blue, red, and white jerseys with blue pants and red and white stripes down the legs. Those games were even more fun because there would be a lot of people in the bleachers and on the sidelines under the tree cooking, eating, and watching the game, but I never saw any of my family there.

Chapter 13

Jobs

After school when I wasn't playing sports, I had jobs to do. I would cut TT's grass or wash her '64 Chevy Impala, and she would give me $5 each time. She was always good to me. When I was younger, she would come get me and take me home with her. She took Par's place after he died because that's what he used to do when he was living. I used to spend the night at her house just as I had at Par's house.

When we moved to New Roads, TT and Dave built a house across the street from us, and I would spend a lot of time there, sometimes falling asleep. He didn't say anything.

When I wasn't playing sports, I would mow lawns in the neighborhood. Everyone would give me $5 except Ms. Jones; she would give me $3 and a bag with a popcorn ball, pecan candy, and a frozen cup; we used to buy our snacks from her.

When I was fourteen, TT used to work at a bar called Four Way. She would take me there when they were closed, and I would help her clean up, sweep, mop, stock the coolers and shelves, and pick up the trash outside. She would give me $20 or $25, and she would let me help myself to a pickled pig's foot and a jumbo soda.

I hid my money in a sock under a bed at TT's house. One day, I counted it up—$106. I put that into a baking powder can and stuck it under the bed. Sometimes, I would work with her two or

three days a week, and I was still cutting grass. Eventually, I started
working with her on Fridays and Saturdays, and at times, it seemed
like I worked all day and night, but she would pay me $100 to $125.

My mother and father knew I was working, so she would ask me
how much TT was paying me. I never told her. She started asking
me to buy cigarettes and cold drinks for her almost every day, and at
times, she would ask me for $5, and I would give it to her. She started
asking for me to buy her pepper sausage and saltine crackers as well
as cigarettes and cold drinks, and I would. I didn't mind because I
had a lot of money. She would tell me to bring back something for
the kids or give them some money so they could go to Ms. Jones for
some pecan candy and bring her back some. I did.

In the summer, TT would take me to work with her Thursdays
through Sundays. I used to work at the gas station as well, and I
would keep the cooler and shelves stocked and cleaned up after they
closed. I was too young to be in the bar when it was open, but she
would let me work the gas pump. Every Sunday night, the owner
would pay me $150 to $200. Oh man, I was making a lot of money.
She would ask me how much I made, but I would just give her $20.
TT would ask me how much I had given her, and I'd tell her.

She said, "Plook, I brought those Buddhas at the flea market.
They're banks. You can put money in them, but you'll have to break
it to get your money out, so make sure you keep some out."

I went to get my money from under the bed. I had $566. I put
$500 in the bank, $20 in my pocket, and the rest back in the baking
powder can and put it back under the bed. I kept asking myself, *Who
am I? Am I supposed to be here? Where am I going?* I still hadn't seen
Jamp or my friends, and I missed them.

Someone who used to come to the bar was selling a motorcycle
for $300. He let me ride it up and down Section Road. I told TT
I wanted to buy it, and she asked me if I had enough for it. I told
her yes, that it was in my Buddha bank. She said, "I told you you'd
have to bust the bottom out of it. I tell you what. I'll pay for it, and
you can pay me back."

I thanked her, and she paid for the bike. She signed some papers the guy had. The next Sunday night, the owner paid me $200, which I gave to TT.

In those days, gas was 25¢ a gallon. I washed the motorcycle and rode it up and down the street all day giving my friends rides.

On Tuesday, TT said, "Let's ride your motorcycle to the club." She got on back, and off we went.

That weekend, the owner paid me $200 again, and I tried to give TT $100, but she said, "Boy, you don't own me nothing. Put it in your bank."

Chapter 14

New Roads

Living in New Roads was fun—I sure didn't miss working in the fields or running the cows over to the dairy to be milked at five in the morning. I had new friends and was able to do so many different things. I was playing football and baseball and running track. I was fourteen then, and I was five-nine and weighed 150. I started lifting weights with some of my JV teammates; I started off bench pressing 100 pounds five times in a row with no problem. They would add more weights to it, and I would lift that also five times with no problem. Finally, I think we got to 160 pounds, which I could lift five times in a row with no problem. One guy asked me if I had ever lifted before. I told him no. I guessed all the work I had done in the fields since I was seven or eight had given me my strength. When I was about eleven or twelve, I was lifting 80-pound bales of hay just like the men would and throwing them on the wagon. I guess working on the plantation wasn't as bad as it seemed back then. I found myself doing things that most kids my age couldn't do. Yep, I was strong and not afraid of anyone or anything.

He always told me, "Boy, you're not to be afraid of anyone. Always look after your sisters and brothers." The only one not there for me to look after was Jamp. Even my brother she had given to her sister to raise lived just across the street.

I couldn't wait for school to start so I could play sports and practice trumpet and drums. When he or she or my sisters and brothers complained about my practicing, I'd do it in the backyard. I was having a lot fun and making plenty of money. On the plantation, I worked all day for $2 but never saw any of it.

Living in New Roads was like living at my Granma and Par's house in the Quarters. My cousins and I would play in the yard all the time while the grown-ups would be sitting on the garry talking, laughing, smoking, drinking beer, wine, cold drinks, or coffee, playing music, and dancing in the yard. They would make us dance with them or for them; they would offer us money to dance, but they would never pay us. They wanted us boys to dance like James Brown. In New Roads, when we used to all get together at TT's house, we would have that same kind of fun with each other.

One time when I was living at Par and Granma's house, they brought me a cowboy outfit—cowboy boots, khaki shorts, white shirt, a blue cowboy hat, and two cap guns in holsters. I was about six or so then, and oh boy, did I have fun! I would shoot you until I couldn't shoot you anymore—*pow pow pow* until all the caps were gone. I'd reload a roll of caps and shoot you with them too. They told me I had to wait until someone went to New Roads before I could get more caps for a nickel a box.

A fruit truck used to come down to the Quarters every day. He sold all kinds of candy, ice cream, fruits, and vegetables, and he would buy pecans. In the backyard was a pecan tree; the grown-ups and even my grandma would be back there picking up pecans and putting them into big sacks. They would give me a little white rice sack, maybe one pound; I remember it had a bird on the side. I'd fill my sack up and tie it up. I'd wait on the garry looking and listening for the truck to come; he would always blow his horn. When I heard him coming down the road, I would run out by the gate and wait for him. One of the grown-ups would say, "Boy, don't you go in that road. You wait for me."

When he got there, I would run to his truck and give him my sack, and he would lean over and give me 25¢. I'd ask him for some caps, and he would give me five boxes, and I would start shooting my gun again. Yep, that's the type of fun we would have when TT moved across the street from us.

Chapter 15

MVP

The summer was almost over, and it had been a good one. I was fourteen, making a lot of money working with TT, and hunting and fishing with Dave. TT started letting me drive home from Erwinville in her car when I wasn't riding my motorcycle, and that was fun. When we were at home sometimes, she would let me drive by myself to the store to get medicine, cigarettes, or something to eat.

It was time to go back to school. my grandparents in California hadn't come yet with their usual gifts of clothes. I gave her $200 so she could buy school clothes for my sisters and brothers. I was happy I had on new clothes that I picked out myself, and she bought new clothes for my sisters and brothers. I ended up giving her another $100 to buy more clothes and shoes. That was the first time we all went to school with new clothes.

My sister was twelve, and she started wanting to comb her own hair; she combed some to the back and some over her face, and she kept looking in the mirror and smiling. She combed our younger sister hair nicely too, and she was smiling in the mirror also. My brothers looked sharp. I was happy because they were happy, and we all walked to school together laughing and playing. At that time, my sister was attending my high school, so we didn't have far to go. I took her to her class and walked to the back of the school, where I watched one of my other sisters and brother walk to the junior high.

They were playing as they walked. I yelled at them to hurry up, and they looked back and waved. I waved back as I walked slowly to my class.

I had tears in my eyes. I lowered my head so the other kids wouldn't see me crying. I was just so happy to see my sisters and brothers with new clothes that made them happy. They had enough new clothes to wear different things every day, and they had a couple of pairs of shoes each too.

While in school, I was still mowing four yards and washing TT's and Dave's cars, and I was working all day on Saturdays. If we didn't finish cleaning up Saturday night, we'd go back on Sundays to finish. TT would give me $100, and I would give my mom half of that so she could buy more clothes for my sisters and brothers. I always had $20 to $40 in my pocket or in my can.

Playing baseball at school was fun; we had three uniforms—one for home games, another for away games, and the third for practice. I played center field and was leadoff batter; I was playing with the big boys. I wished Jamp and my other friends from the Quarters could see me. It was fun, but it was different from how we played in the Quarters. We had umpires—one behind the plate, another at first base, and another at third base. We had those white chalked boxes we stood in at the plate. Our away games took us to Livonia, St. Francisville, Morganza, and Bachelor. I would come home sometimes with my legs, knees, and hips hurting and bloody from sliding, but I was definitely having fun.

My coach gave me shorts to wear under my baseball pants to help keep me from ripping open my scrapes, but they didn't help that much. My coach told me it was all part of the game, so I learned to play with my scrapes and bruises. I got more scars playing baseball than I did playing football. It didn't matter how badly I was hurting when I got home—I still had homework to do, and I had to help my sisters and brothers with theirs. I was still an honor student, and I even helped some of my friends with their homework. But at least I wasn't working in the fields, feeding animals, or watering the garden.

But there was still no one who would call me "Son" at my games. My teammates would pat my back and say, "Good game!" but never my parents or brothers or sisters. Game after game, week after week, he never showed up. It was the same with football. I would look and listen for their voices but would never hear them. Sometimes, I would walk home from games slowly so I could get all my tears out before I got home. I'd walk in with my head down so they couldn't see my red eyes. Yes, he and she would be there. I would go to my room and start my homework and help my sisters and brothers with theirs.

That didn't stop me from playing with my friends, and they complimented me on my abilities; I guess I was pretty good at sports. At the end of the season, we had a banquet for the baseball team in the gym, and I told him and her when it was. I walked with two friends to the gym; we were laughing and talking. Right outside the gym, my coach asked me where my tie was. I pulled my tie out of my pocket and gave it to him. He tied it for me. Yep, I had asked him before I left the house to tie it for me, but he said he didn't know how to tie one. I had on a black suit, white shirt, black shoes, and a black tie that I had bought from the store back of town.

The coach wanted us all to dress up with black suits and ties; he said we looked sharp. He asked if my family was there, but I said nothing. Once again, my eyes began to tear up. I wiped them as I walked into the gym. I started looking for them, but I knew they weren't coming.

Jack, our best pitcher, asked me what was wrong. I said, "Nothing." He said, "Cheer up and smile. This is going to be a good night for you." I tried, but tears came back to my eyes. After the banquet had been going on for about forty-five minutes, the coach announced that the team had gotten together and had chosen the MVP for that year. He said, "Our center fielder, Plook," and everyone cheered and clapped. I went up to receive the award, and everyone was saying, "Speech!" but I hadn't expected to receive an award, and I didn't know what to say.

I looked around again but still didn't see them. I simply thanked my coaches and teammates. All the others who had received awards and done the same, but they also thanked their parents for their support. I couldn't say that.

I got back to the table, and Jack was standing and clapping for me. He said, "I told you this was going to be a good night for you!" We hugged, and I didn't want to let go of him because I didn't want him to see me cry. Even though something important was missing, I was happy my teammates and coaches thought I was that year's MVP. The tears I was shedding became tears of joy at least for the time being.

Baseball was over, so I tried basketball, but I was just too short. I stayed on the honor roll, however, even though I was cutting grass, washing cars, and working Saturdays and sometimes Sundays with TT. I was happy that I was able to afford new clothes for my brothers and sisters.

One Sunday night when TT and I were coming home from Four Way in Erwinville, we were on False River Road. It was dark, probably around nine or ten. I looked for Jamp and my friends as we passed the Quarters, but it was too dark. I asked TT, "Do you know if my brother Jamp still live down in the Quarters?"

She said, "I think so, but I don't know. When was the last time you saw him?"

"About four years ago, but not since I stopped going to St. Alma's when we were living on Lodio."

"It's been that long?"

"Yes ma'am."

"I'll ask somebody from the Quarters the next time I see one if he still lives down there, but I don't think anyone lives down there anymore. We go to church at Little Zion now."

I didn't say anything. The next thing I knew, we were pulling up in the yard. Here came Jojo, her big, brown bulldog that always jumped around and wagged his tail when he saw her come home. Some of my cousins from Texas were living with her; my aunt had died, and her children had come to live with TT. I had a bedroom over there, but there were five of them. I let my cousin sleep in my bed in the room with Uncle Snow.

The next day was a school day, so I talked for only about ten minutes. I was waiting for them to leave the front room so I could put my money in my bank. No one knew that the Buddha was my bank except for TT and Dave. TT asked me to come into her bedroom, which was in the back of the house down the hallway. She said, "Don't look like they'll be moving too soon from the living room." She handed me the green money bag she used to take the money to the bank from the club. She unlocked it, and I put $200 in it. She locked it, put it in her closet, and gave me the key. I put the key in my pocket, said goodnight, and walked home just across the street.

I walked in, and she came out of her room. "How much you made today? Give me ten dollars." I simply gave her a $10. She said my sisters and brothers needed lunch money, so I gave her $3 or $4 more.

One day, I drove my brother on the back of my motorcycle to the store. I brought both of us black cowboy boots, blue jeans, belts with big buckles, and cowboys shirts with horses on the pockets. His was red, and mine was black. We looked like cowboys that morning going to school.

The next morning when we were getting dressed for school, he came out of the bathroom with the same outfit on. I told him he couldn't wear those same clothes again. Oh did he start to fuss and cry. He refused to take his clothes off. Even she couldn't get him to change his clothes. I told him he should at least change his shirt. He raced out the door, and she said I should let him go. He ran all the way to school.

The next week when I got paid, I brought him a pair of black and white jeans and two more cowboy shirts—a black one and a blue one. That was another time when I was so happy to see them happy.

One of my Texas cousins was graduating from Rosenwald and wanted to visit Southern University. TT was going to take her, and she invited me along. The school was about forty minutes away. We were stopped at a red light just before the turn-in to the campus when *Bam!* A car rear-ended us. TT was hurt when she hit her stomach on the steering wheel. She was pregnant. The trunk had a big dent. The police asked her if she needed medical help or an ambulance, but she said no.

But then after we visited campus, she said she wasn't feeling well and wanted to go to the doctor. My cousin didn't know how to drive, so I drove us to the hospital. After we were there for a couple of hours, they told her that she and the baby were okay, so I drove us home.

About two months later, she had delivered the baby and had started back at work. One Saturday night, TT and I were driving home from work along the levee about midnight. As we came around a curve, a car coming toward us had its brights on. TT said she couldn't see; she kept flashing her brights hoping they would turn theirs off. I couldn't see the road either. She slowed down. The closer we got, the brighter the lights got. We saw a man standing in the middle of the road waving his hands. All of a sudden *Bam!* She grabbed my head and pushed it down. There was a big black cow standing in front of us. We both ducked. the man asked, "Are y'all all right?" TT asked me if I was okay. I said yes and asked her if she was okay. She said yes. The man told us not to move. The cow was on top of the hood; its legs had come through the windshield. As we were leaning over, my back started to hurt. I felt something on my shoulder when I tried to get up.

The guy got her out of the car by hooking a chain to the car door. I was scared and started to cry. The man told me, "Don't move, boy. I'm going to get you out." I heard him doing something with the chain. Then I heard chains clinking and his tires spinning on the road. I smelled rubber burning. The car started to rock back and forth. Then a big kick. It seemed that something went over my head.

He came back to the car and got me out through the windshield. He said, "I'll be damned. That damn cow was knocked out."

I watched this huge, seven- or eight-hundred-pound cow limp across the road. TT was sitting on the ground bent over and saying her head was hurting badly. The car was totaled. The engine was on the ground. TT passed out, but she was okay and so was I. The guy took his truck and pulled her car to the side of the road; he gave us a ride home thank God.

Chapter 16

Lots of Crawfish

The next week, school was out for Christmas break. One Monday morning, my uncle Dave came over and asked me to go to Baton Rouge with him. I went inside and told her. She asked, "Where y'all going there?" I said, "I don't know." She said, "Bring me back a cold drink and a pack of cigarettes."

Uncle Dave and I drove to Baton Rouge, somewhere I had never been before. We went to this place to pick up some cases of meat, we went to a fruit stand to get some vegetables, and we drove to where he worked. I helped him unload everything, and he showed me around the building. We put the meat in a big refrigerator and drove home.

The next day, we went to a place not far from where he worked and picked up sacks and sacks of crawfish. We went to where he worked, and he had these big pots of water, maybe three or four of them, with burners underneath.

Once the water started to boil, he put in all types of seasonings and a sack of crawfish in each one. We must have been there six hours or so. I was drinking cold drinks while he was drinking whiskey. When we finished boiling all the crawfish, we put them in three or four big ice chests, and I helped him carry them upstairs. We left and went home, and he gave me $40.

The next week, he asked me to go with him again. We did the same thing—on Monday, we picked up meat and vegetables, and on Tuesday, the crawfish. No one else was there because they were closed on Mondays and Tuesdays.

But that Tuesday, he had a private party to work, and someone who was supposed to help him couldn't make it. He asked me if I wanted to work with him. I said, "Yes sir. What do you need me to do?" He went up front and got a white book with all the items on the menu, and he showed me how to fill out the menu ticket. He said, "Tonight, there will be only three items they can choose. Draw one line for each person who orders that item. If five people order the same thing, put down four lines and a fifth one that crosses them."

He gave me an apron, a white jacket, and a white hat. He said we would work only about three or four hours. I worked with four other people, and my uncle paid me $85.

That following Monday, we went to Baton Rouge and did the same thing again. My uncle asked me how old I was. I told him fourteen.

"When will you be fifteen?"

"In March."

"You think you'd like doing this type of work? I want you to be my backup waiter—twenty-five bucks a day plus tips, maybe fifty or a hundred a night."

I still had one more week left before we went back to school.

He said, "I want you to work on Thursday."

We left for work about nine that morning. We stopped at the store for some pepper sausage, bread, and moon cakes because we couldn't eat the food at the restaurant. He picked up two more men, and we drove to the job.

I was inside helping Dave fold napkins when—my God! My brother Jamp came walking through the door! We hugged each other for a long time. He told me he was one of the cooks. Dave asked, "Y'all know each other?" We told him we were brothers. We talked every time we got a chance. I was so happy to see him!

The next Monday, he came to New Roads, and we walked all over. I can't remember who dropped him off or who came back to get him. He was going to Rougon High. We spend as much time as we could together.

When I turned fifteen, I bought a brand-new motorcycle in Baton Rouge. I rode it everywhere, even all the way down to Cherrie Quarters, where Jamp was still living. One day, my motorcycle was repossessed for nonpayment. She would tell me the guy from the motorcycle place called and said he needed the payments. Every time I would ask him about it, he would say he would take care of it, but he never did, and the man came and took my motorcycle back. But somehow, Jamp would visit me. One time, we went to a store in town and bought matching outfits—we looked like twins.

One day, my father told me that two men couldn't live in the same house and that he wasn't leaving. I had had about $3,200 in the bank; he paid $1,500 for the motorcycle. After the man took my motorcycle, I went to the bank and found out that he had taken it all about two months earlier and had closed the account. I was mad. I asked him what had happened to my money, but again, he said two men couldn't live in the same house and he wasn't leaving. He said I better get my attitude together.

I never saw any of the money I had worked so hard for. It seemed that he wanted me around only for the money I was earning. When I would come home after working, they always asked me how much I had earned. At first, I would tell them, and they would ask for most of it. One time, TT paid me about $65 or $70, and he asked me for it. I did, and he gave me $20 back. And then she asked for $20 or $30 for something I can't remember. I told her to ask Daddy to give it to her out of my money, and she said, "Boy, he done spent that money. I bet you'll never see it again." I said that was my money.

When he came home from work, I asked him to give Mama $30 of my money, and he asked, "What money?" I told him that he had $210 of my money, and he said, "Boy, you better go outside and play!" I started to cry. I wondered why he was treating me like that. *Is this how it's supposed to be?*

I told TT about it, and she got mad as hell. That was when I started hiding my money at her house. After that, when I would come home from working with TT and he would ask me for my pay, I would tell him TT hadn't paid me yet. He didn't say anything, but I could see the mad look in his eyes like he was looking straight through me. My knees started knocking. He balled up his fist and went to his room. He slammed the door so hard that it broke. He came out of his room and didn't say anything. I was trying to figure all this out. *Why do I have to leave home? Why does he treat me like this? Why do I have to leave my sisters and brothers?*

It got worse. She started doing the same thing. I would be so tired after working ten to twelve hours with Dave and getting home around midnight. She'd ask me for whatever food she had asked me to bring her, and she would ask for $5 or $10, which I would give her. I would count my money at work, so I knew how much I had, but in the morning, my pants were lighter; I knew someone had been through my pockets because I would have probably just $10 to $20 left. Half of my money was gone, but no one would admit to taking it. That happened to me almost every time I didn't hide my money at TT's. I was afraid to ask him about it, so I didn't say anything.

One night, I couldn't get to sleep. I saw my mother going through my pockets and asked, "Why are you in my pockets?" She said, "I'm your mother. I can go in your pockets whenever I want. Where's your money?" I didn't answer her.

I tried my best to always help my family, but even my brother stole from me. One time, I had just spent money on clothes for all my sisters and brothers, and I gave my parents $20 each. I still had about $200, but again, I woke up and checked my wallet—all my money was gone. I was mad. I asked them, "Why do y'all keep stealing from me?" I was crying. I told them I was leaving and wasn't coming back. I went to TT's house and told them about that. I could hear my mother and father fussing with each other and asking each other, "Did you take his money?" They both denied it.

My brother who lived with TT and Dave said that one of our brothers was in the backyard digging a hole, so Daddy went into the backyard and saw some fresh dirt. He dug up a coffee can, and there was all the money—$200—that my brother had stolen. It looked like I could never do anything right. I had just bought school clothes for all of them, but everyone kept stealing from me. I had to leave. I couldn't stay there anymore. I started staying with TT and Dave.

One day, TT was on the phone with my grandmother in California. I asked my grandmother if I could come and live with her. She said, "No, not now. There's no room for you. Maybe later when there's room."

I asked TT to call my uncle who lived in Texas and ask him if I could go live with him. He said yes, so I told him I would be there in about a month after I had saved up some money.

When the time came for me to move to Texas, I told my father and mother that I was leaving. He asked me how I was going to get there, and I showed him my bus ticket. He took it and tore it up and walked back to his room. I walked to TT and Dave's house and told her what had happened, and she said I could stay with them.

Chapter 17

Off to California

A couple of weeks later, TT told me that she had talked with my grandmother; she had agreed to take me in. I worked for a few more weeks to save up for a bus ticket to California.

One Tuesday morning after he had left for work, I hugged my mother and kissed her goodbye. I told my sisters and brothers goodbye, grabbed my suitcase, and walked over to TT and Dave's house. They were sitting under the car porch drinking coffee and smoking cigarettes. I told them goodbye, and TT started to cry. Dave also had tears in his eyes, and I started to cry too, but I knew I had to be strong. This was something I had to do. I couldn't live there any longer.

TT offered to drive me to the bus station. I looked across the street and saw my mother, sisters, and brothers in the yard. My mother was smoking. I couldn't tell if she was happy or sad. I told her goodbye again, and she just looked at me and told me to take care of myself. I said, "Yes ma'am, I will." I told her I loved her and my sisters and brothers. None of them showed any reaction.

I got in TT's car and waved goodbye to them one last time. Tears were running down my face. They waved back. TT's hands were shaking and her lips were quivering; tears were rolling down her face; she drove very slowly. We didn't have far to go, maybe a mile or so. I had plenty of time before the bus was leaving. She was looking straight ahead. In a shaking voice, she said, "You don't have to go. You can live with me. I'll ask them to give you to me. I promise you he won't hurt you anymore. Please change your mind and stay with us. You already have your own bed over here, and I'll build you your own room."

With tears rolling down my face, I said, "I have to go. I know you love me and would take care of me and not let anything happen to me, but I have to go."

We got to the bus station, and the driver put my suitcase in the bus luggage compartment. TT and I hugged each other; we were both crying. She didn't want to let me go. She kept saying, "Please don't leave me." I told her, "I love you. Take care of yourself. Don't worry about me. I'll be all right."

She asked, "How much money do you have?" When I told her about $1,500, she went into her purse and stuck some money in my pocket. She told me that if I needed anything, I should call her. She said, "If you don't like it in California and you're not being treated right, call me and I'll send for you."

The bus driver asked, "Boy, are you going to California?"

"Yes sir."

"Okay, it's time to get on the bus."

TT and I hugged each other again. I said one more time, "I love you, and thank you for all you have done for me."

I pulled myself away from her and got on the bus. I saw her looking at me and waving goodbye, and I waved back as the bus drove off. I saw her holding onto the car as she was walking around to get in; her legs were weak. I was crying even more. I looked back until I couldn't see her anymore. I wondered, *Where am I going? Am I supposed to go there?* I wanted someone to love me just as my teammates had people who loved them. *Will there ever be anyone else like her who will stand up against him for me as I know she did?*

I was fifteen. The last person who had said he loved me was Par; he used to tell me that all the time, but I had never heard that from my mother or father. TT showed me how much she loved me and would miss me, and that was what I wanted to hear from my parents. I started wondering if I was really their son. They would talk to me only when they thought I had money. I was tired of them stealing my money. She would say, "TT isn't your mother. She can't tell you what to do with your money." He had stopped asking me for money; I guessed that was because he had taken enough from me, maybe $3,000.

I started to calm down and stopped crying. The bus stopped in Lake Charles, and I was in the bus station café. The driver had told me my next bus would leave in four hours. I ordered a hamburger, fries, and a soda. I put my hand into my pocket and felt more money than I knew I had put there. I had had only $10 in there; the rest was in my socks. I went to the rest room, got into a stall, and counted the money TT had given me—eight $100 bills and ten $20 bills. I cried. No one had ever done that for me.

I realized how much she loved me, and I thought about going back and living with her and Dave because I knew they loved me. I had left them behind, and I knew I would miss Jamp, who I had lost track of for three or four years. We had been reunited for just a year. I had had a good job, so I hadn't needed to ask my mother or father for anything, not that he ever would have given me or my brothers or sisters anything.

I thought about going back and keeping track of my brothers and sisters from across the street at TT's house, where I would live with my brother and still be able to see Jamp, whom I had started calling Will.

Chapter 18

On the Road

I heard the bus driver announce we were in Houston. I thought about getting off the bus there because my uncle there had told me I could live with him. But the bus driver knew that I was only fifteen and that this was my first time traveling. He got my luggage and led me to my next bus; there must have been twenty or so buses. The driver of my next bus loaded my suitcase and told me to get on. We drove off; I had had no time to call my uncle or even put much thought into it.

I fell asleep; the next thing I knew was that the driver said we were in San Antonio. The trip to California would take three days, so I had plenty of time to wonder, *Am I doing the right thing? Am I going where I'm supposed to be? What will California be like?*

We got to Phoenix, where I stayed for about three or four hours. Again, I bought a hamburger, fries, and soda and sat in the waiting room. I started to get a little scared when I saw people begging for money and cigarettes; they weren't very clean, but then again, I hadn't taken a shower in two days.

I had never seen so many different people, and I couldn't understand what some of them were saying when they spoke to me. A woman with three kids sat by me; I thought they were Indians. She spoke to them in a language I didn't understand, but she spoke to me in English. She wanted to know my name, where I had come from, and where I was going. She and her children were eating potato chips.

After about an hour or so, two of the kids started to cry, and she tried to get them to be quiet, but they wouldn't stop crying. I asked her to watch my suitcase, and I went to the washroom and bought a candy bar. One of her children stood in front of me with his hand out; he was crying and saying something I couldn't understand, but I knew he was asking me for some of my candy. I asked the woman if I could share my candy with her children, and she said yes. She told me she had spent the last of her money on the potato chips. They were going to Bakersfield to live with her mother; she had just broken up with her husband.

I gave the candy to one of her kids, and another one snatched it out of his hand. She split up the candy bar and gave a piece to each one. That kept them quiet for about fifteen minutes. One of them came and stood in front of me again saying something I didn't understand, but I knew he was hungry. It was about an hour before my bus was leaving, so I asked her to watch my suitcase again and went to the café. I ordered burgers, fries, and sodas for the woman and her three children, which cost about $7. I asked the woman to come over and tell the waitress what they wanted on their burgers. Man, they ate their meals as if they hadn't eaten in a long time. In about twenty minutes or so, they were all snoozing on the bench. One of her kids rested his head on my arm and went to sleep.

When we got on the bus, the little kid wanted to sit next to me. She was sitting across from me with one kid in her lap; he seemed to be about two or three. The other, who was about six, was sitting next to her. The kid next to me fell asleep, and I did to.

When I woke up, I asked her where we were, and she said somewhere in California. We stopped around eight at night. The driver told me we would get to Vallejo about nine the next night. We stayed there for about an hour and a half. I gave her $20 so she and the kids could eat. She went to the café and came back with a couple of bags of chicken, fries, and bread. They offered me some, but I had ordered a hamburger and fries and was waiting for my number to be called. She tried to give me change from the $20, but I told her to keep it.

Again, I saw people of many different races speaking languages I didn't understand. They didn't look like white people. I guessed they were Indians or Orientals, who I had only read about or seen on television. I thought maybe they were mulattos because it sounded like they were speaking Creole.

I wondered if my grandparents would like me; I wondered how they would treat me. *Will they love me? What about my uncles and aunts?* My grandmother had told me that I was about the same age as one of them and older than two of them. I hoped they would let me stay.

My grandmother had told me to call her when I got to Vallejo. I kept seeing these big mountains everywhere I looked. I had never seen anything like that in Louisiana of course.

When we got to Bakersfield, the woman gave me a hug and thanked me for everything. The kids hugged me too. I went to the waiting area, and it was as hot there as it was outside. The bus driver told me to listen for the announcement of my next bus, and he gave me a piece of paper with the number of my bus written on it.

I boarded the bus, and we left Bakersfield. We stopped every four or five hours, and the driver would let us off for thirty minutes or an hour. The closer I got to Vallejo, the more nervous I became. I didn't know anyone there but my grandparents, and I couldn't quite remember what they looked like other than that my grandmother was very short, light skinned, and beautiful. My grandfather was very tall, big, and dark skinned with a deep voice. I hadn't seen any of them in a couple of years. I wondered if my uncle would play ball with me as he used to when he came to Louisiana. He was always nice to me; he would always give me a $1 or a $5 and tell me to put it in my bank. That was how I could buy candy at school like the rest of the kids did. I thought he wouldn't have to go to Louisiana anymore to see me. I wanted to show him how fast I could run, catch balls, and bat. I hoped I could play sports in California and hear them cheering for me. So many things were going through my mind as I got closer to Vallejo.

Chapter 19

Vallejo, California

I heard the bus driver say, "Vallejo." He stopped, and I got off. He handed me my suitcase. The bus station was closed. Others who had gotten off the bus with me were getting into cars. I found a phone booth and called them. My grandmother answered, and I said, "This is Ernest. I'm here at the bus station." She said, "We'll be there in a few minutes."

Thirty minutes went by. An hour passed. Then two hours. I called her again at about midnight. She said, "Where are you? We couldn't find you! Are you sure you're in Vallejo?" I was scared and nervous. "Yes ma'am. That's what the bus driver said." She told me to ask the clerk where I was. I told her that the bus station was closed. She told me they had just been to the bus station, and it wasn't closed. I felt lost. My uncle got on the phone and told me to look for a street sign. I did. "Yes sir, it says McDonald Avenue." I heard him tell someone that I was at the bus station in Richmond. He told me they would be there in thirty minutes. "Don't talk to anybody. Stay where there's plenty of light. We'll be driving a white car."

My legs were weak. I was scared. I saw women standing and walking around with very few clothes on. I was afraid to look at them. They would walk over to cars that would stop and talk to the drivers. At least two women asked me if I wanted to have a good time, and I said no. I had never seen anything like that before. I

didn't know what to do. I was afraid to look at them, so I kept looking at the ground. I wondered why the bus driver hadn't taken me to
Vallejo. I hoped my grandparents weren't mad at me for getting off
the bus at the wrong place and making them drive farther to get me.

After what I thought was an hour, I looked at my watch; only fifteen minutes had gone by. I spotted a long, white car coming toward
me slowly. The people inside were looking at me. The car stopped,
and a man rolled down his window. "Are you Ernest?" I said yes. My
uncle was driving, and my grandmother was in the passenger seat.
He got out, shook my hand, and put my suitcase in the trunk. He
opened the back door for me. I said, "I'm sorry I got off the bus at
the wrong place." She said that was okay as long as I was fine.

My uncle told me that Richmond was a place that I didn't want
to be, which made me even more scared and nervous. I wondered,
*What am I getting myself into? Are there bad people in California? Why
did he say that Vallejo and Richmond people didn't like each other?
Will they like people from Louisiana?* He and I talked as we drove.
My grandmother didn't say much other than she was happy I had
made it safely.

At their house, I met two more uncles and my aunt. My grandmother asked me if I was hungry. I said, "No ma'am." I was very
hungry, but it was almost two in the morning. I thought I had
caused enough trouble for one day, and I knew she was tired. I asked
for just a glass of water. My uncle showed me to the back bedroom
and pulled out a rollaway bed. He gave me some covers and a pillow.
I stuck my suitcase into the closet after getting some underwear out
of it. I took a shower and went to bed. I had made it to Vallejo, but
I kept waking up throughout the night because one or both of my
uncles were snoring so loudly that I couldn't sleep. But everyone
seemed nice. That was when I became Ernest; no one there knew
me as Plook.

The next day, one of my uncles took me to a McDonalds. When
we got there, I looked for a sign that read Colored, but I didn't see
one. He just walked in through the front door, turned around, and

asked me what was wrong. "Come on in," he said. I didn't know what to say. We ordered food to go, and as we drove home, he asked me why I had looked afraid to go in. I told him that in Louisiana, black people weren't allowed to go into the front door of a restaurant, that only white people were allowed to do that. I said, "We always had to go to the window that said Colored."

Man, did he laugh. "Are you telling me the truth?"

I said yes, that that was the way it was in the South.

When we got back to the house, he told Grandma what had happened, and she explained to them that that was how it was in the South. That uncle had never been to Louisiana before. They laughed and teased me about it for some time, and they asked me a lot about Louisiana.

We ate, and I got up from the table and walked into the living room. I looked through this big picture window and saw a beautiful girl—tall, light skinned, with a big afro. I had no idea who she was, but I asked God to make her my wife. I asked the others who she was, but by that time, she was out of sight. We opened the door and looked down the street. There she was. "That's Lorraine. She lives two houses down," I was told.

Later that day, my uncle and I were outside; he was introducing me to everyone we met. I didn't catch on at first, but after a couple of times, I noticed that he was calling me his brother. I turned around and there she was standing two feet away from me. Man, she was even more beautiful close-up. My legs got weak. He introduced me to her, and all I could say was hi. She had a big smile. I knew that as fine as she was, she must have a boyfriend already and that I had no chance of making her my girlfriend. But I would see her every day in the street, on the corner, or in our garage. Everyone met on the corner to talk and laugh. When she was around, I could never take my eyes off her.

One day, I got the courage to ask her out on a date. She laughed and said, "No, I'm only twelve." I thought she was lying; I was sure she had a boyfriend. I thought, *What have they been feeding that girl*

up here? She must be from Louisiana or somewhere else down South.
She didn't want to date me, but when we started school, she and her
brother and I would walk there together. They attended junior high
while I went to senior high with my uncle.

One day, I was called to the office and was told they needed
a copy of my transcripts and transfer papers from my school in
Louisiana. All I had was my report card. I called my mother and told
her I needed her to go to the office and sign the papers so they could
mail my transcripts to California, and she said she would.

Two weeks later on a Monday, my teacher told me to go to the
office. They said they needed my paperwork by Friday. The secretary
asked me for my parents' phone number; she called and told my
mom she had to have my transcripts before Friday or they would
have to put me back in ninth grade until they received it. The secretary told me that my mom had said she would take care of it.

Come Monday, I was told that the school hadn't received my
transcripts. They took my books, and the principal told the secretary to take me over to the junior high. I ended up in ninth grade
again and was bored because I had been taught all the same stuff
in Louisiana. I wondered, *Why are my parents treating me like this?*
Why don't they love me? What did I do wrong? Why didn't they send
my paperwork? Our place in Louisiana was so close to the school; it
would have taken her just five minutes to walk there.

That was how things were going for me, but everything wasn't
all bad; I had the chance to see Lorraine more in junior high. She
was a cheerleader, and I started to play sports on all the A teams
in junior high. I saw her cheering or sitting in the bleachers or on
the sidelines with my uncle or others from the neighborhood when
I played football and basketball. After games, we would all walk
home together and sometimes stop at Pluto's for hot dogs. I became
friends with her brother, mother, aunt, uncle, and stepfather; we
used to laugh and talk all the time. Her mother was from Louisiana,
and we talked about that state all the time. I told her that Lorraine

and I were becoming friends but weren't boyfriend and girlfriend. She and I became closer, and I talked to her family even more. Her family used to always ask me if I liked Lorraine. I guessed her mother could see how I looked at her. I told her mother that I had asked her out once but she had said no. Her mother told me to keep asking her, but I couldn't figure out why she said that. I said, "Yes ma'am, I will." I guessed she knew Lorraine's brother wouldn't be there for her if anyone ever tried to hurt her.

She and I were becoming better friends; I wanted it to be more than a friendship, but I respected her and was happy just to be her friend. I started looking after her as if she were my little sister. We'd laugh and talk with each other, and she knew I'd do anything for her and even give her money with no strings attached. I never tried to kiss her or anything like that, and if I saw her at a party, I wouldn't even ask her to dance. But one thing for sure—she knew I wouldn't let anything happen to her or let anyone disrespect her; anyone who did would have to deal with me. I believed her mother was confident that I'd never let anything happen to her; she would always tell me to look after her, and I would look her in the eyes and say, "Ms. Thelma, don't worry. I'll always look after her and her brothers too."

One day, she asked me, "When was the last time you asked her out?" I wasn't bold enough to ask her again because I didn't want to lose our friendship. Her aunt said, "Keep asking her. If you were a little older or if I were a little younger, you wouldn't have to ask me twice." Ms. Thelma said, "Not if I saw him first. You wouldn't stand a chance."

I laughed. Everyone would always ask me, "Is she your girl-friend?" or "Y'all together?" I would always say, "No, but if she were, you'd know it. She's only my friend, but you better respect her." I guessed we were closer to each other than we thought.

So far in Vallejo, everything was going pretty well even if it was a whole lot different from Louisiana. The school was big; there were a lot of kids there of many different races and nationalities, but everybody got along with each other. I saw black guys kissing and hugging on white and Asian girls, something they'd be beaten or jailed for in Louisiana and maybe even killed. Yes, it looked as if they didn't have racial problems there, but boy was I wrong.

Chapter 20

Riot

The week after I had been sent to junior high, I was in the restroom zipping my pants up when all of a sudden out of nowhere this white boy hit me upside my head and said, "You nigger! I'll kill you!" He swung at me again but missed. I can't say we had a fight. He'd hit me once, but I hit him three or four times in the face. He ran out of the washroom, I chased him, and he fell down in the hallway. I walked the other way to find my uncle. I didn't know what was going on; there were fights going on all over the place in the hallways and classrooms. I wanted to see my uncle and find out what was going on. Someone grabbed me from behind and threw me up against the wall. As I came off the wall, I started punching him until he fell. Someone yelled, "That was the vice principal you just hit!" I had been at the school for only a couple of days, so I hadn't known that.

Someone said there was a riot going on between the black and the white students. I didn't see anyone I knew. I just wanted to make sure my uncle was okay. Someone grabbed me from behind again and pushed me up against the wall. I heard someone talking on a radio. Two policemen took me to the office and told me to sit and not move. "If you do, we'll arrest you and take you to jail."

A short white man standing behind the counter with the police and two or three other people were talking; I couldn't hear what they were saying, but they kept looking my way as if I had just done something wrong. An ambulance left the school. The short white guy was showing the police his face. He had a swollen eye and mouth, and his glasses were broken. A woman handed him a bag of ice for his eye. A police officer asked me what we had been fighting about. I said, "Sir, I don't know. I've been here for only a couple of days."

I told him how I had been called a nigger by someone in the washroom who had punched me and threatened to kill me. I said that I had punched him and had chased him out into the hallway, that someone had come up from behind and had pushed me up against the wall, and that I turned and punched him. I asked the officer, "Can I go find my uncle?" He said, "You're not going anywhere." He asked me for my parents' phone number, and I explained I was living with my grandparents. I said that I had just moved there from Louisiana and that my grandmother was at work.

He cuffed me to the chair and left. At that point of course, I knew who the vice principal was; he was glaring at me as he held the bag of ice to his eye. He came from behind the counter, stood in front of me, and said, "You'll never come back to this school!"

It seemed that they had me sit there for almost four hours. Another officer came in, and I told him I needed to go to the washroom. He uncuffed me and walked with me to the restroom; he stood by my side the whole time I was there. I was wondering, *What am I doing here? Am I supposed to be here? Maybe I should have stayed in Louisiana with TT and Dave.* It seemed like everything my father had said was starting to come true; he had said I'd end up in jail and never amount to anything.

The police said they were taking me to the police station until someone picked me up. I hadn't started that fight. I hadn't done anything wrong. I didn't want to come here and be a problem for my grandparents. I was afraid they'd send me back to Louisiana. I started to pray even though I didn't know how to pray or even if God would hear me: *God, please don't let them take me to jail, be kicked out of school, or let my grandmother send me back to Louisiana. I have never been involved in anything like this before. I've seen stuff like this only on TV. God, I've never been at a school where all these different races are. How did I get here? Why did I come to a place where people don't like me?*

In Louisiana, whites and blacks went to separate schools. I wondered why black and white students fought each other. I hoped my grandmother would send me to an all-black school. I didn't want to go back to Louisiana, and I didn't want to get into fights at school. Before I had traveled to California, I marched with the NAACP for the same thing—to get blacks and whites to go to school together, but that didn't happen when I was there. At that point, I was glad school integration hadn't happened. All I kept hearing was that this was a riot. I asked myself, *What's a riot?* I wanted my uncle, Lorraine, or her brother to tell me what in the hell was going on.

Hours later, a police officer uncuffed me and told me to go home and not come back to school until they had gotten in touch with my grandmother. I walked into the hallway. I didn't see anyone. I was scared to death that I'd be sent back to Louisiana. I had only tried to protect myself. I decided to call my uncle in Houston if my grandmother told me to go back to Louisiana.

That evening, I saw a police officer walking up to our house. I opened the door before he knocked and asked, "Yes sir, can I help you?"

He asked, "Is your grandmother home?"

I told him she was due home very shortly. Just then, she pulled up, and she and the officer spoke outside. I was afraid she'd be mad at me and tell me to start packing without hearing my side of the story. My uncle, who was standing beside me looking out the window, asked, "Man, what happened?" I told him I had gotten into a fight. "Are you the one who hit the vice principal?" I told him the whole story.

My grandmother came in with the police officer. I saw that she was mad. She told my uncle to go to his room and told me to sit at the kitchen table. She and the officer sat there. I hadn't seen that officer at the school. He asked me what had happened, and I told him the full story about being attacked in the washroom, running out into the hallway, being pushed up against the wall, and hitting someone who turned out to be the vice principal. He said I couldn't leave the house. He told my grandmother that they weren't going to charge me with anything yet because they didn't know what to charge me with. He said they had to wait and see if he made it out of the hospital; he wasn't breathing on his own. He was in a coma—I had no idea what he was talking about. He told my grandmother that he or another officer might come back and arrest me.

She was looking at me as he left. I started to cry; I told her that I was sorry, that I hadn't started the fight. I begged her not to send me back to Louisiana. I didn't think about what he had said about taking me to jail; I just didn't want to go back to my mother and father.

She looked at me and called my uncle out of his room. She asked him if he knew what had happened in school. He said there was supposed to have been a riot. She told me to tell her the whole truth, and with tears rolling down my face, I did. She told my uncle to call his brother who was a police officer, and tell him to come over.

About ten minutes later, he arrived. I told him the whole story just as it had happened. He said he was going to the station to find out what was going on. Grandma couldn't take off until Tuesday to go to school.

Someone called on Saturday evening and told my grandmother that Steve, the kid I had fought, was talking and that there would be no charges filed against me. But they said I still couldn't go back to school. She told me she wasn't sending me back to Louisiana. She said, "TT has already told me that you and your father don't get along."

I said, "Thank you so much, Grandma!" My tears were flowing. I hugged her and again told her how sorry I was and that I'd never do that again. She looked up at me not cracking a smile and said, "You don't never let nobody hit you for nothing and get away with it. I'll never be mad at you for protecting yourself. You just don't never be out there starting any trouble." I told her I wouldn't.

I asked her what black-only school I could go to, and she said there were no segregated schools there. My uncle asked me if there were all-black schools in Louisiana, and I told him yes. "You saying all the blacks go to their own schools, all the whites go to their own schools, and other nationalities and races have their own schools?" I said, "No, man. We don't have all these different people in Louisiana. You're either white or black." He had never known that. I told him I had never seen anyone who wasn't white or black before I got on the bus to come to California. Grandma smiled at that.

She said, "Baby, you're not going to find no school down here like that, but don't worry about that. You'll be fine. I'll take care of all this on Tuesday."

All that happened when I was just fifteen and had been in junior high for only a few days.

Chapter 21

Back in School

When Tuesday arrived, Grandma drove my uncle and me to school and told us to have a good day. My uncle walked to his class. Grandma asked me where my class was. I asked, "I don't have to go to the office with you?"

"For what?" she asked. "I don't need your help. You've done enough already. You go to class. This isn't my first time here. I'll take care of this."

I said, "Yes ma'am," and I walked to class.

The teacher asked me where my note was. I asked, "What note?" She said, "The note from the office."

I told her no one had given me a note. She just told me to take my seat.

No one said anything to me all day. I went home, and when my grandma came home, she asked me how my day had gone. "Did anyone bother you? Did the principal or anyone else say anything to you?"

I said, "No ma'am, it went fine."

She had that look in her eyes that said she meant business. She was very short, but she wasn't afraid of anything. She said, "I've been up there before for two of my children, and they know I don't play. They know me very well, and they know not to mess with my kids especially if they haven't done anything wrong."

I told her I'd never started any problems with anyone.

She just said, "Finish your homework."

Man, was that a relief. My eyes teared up. I was so happy to be back in school again. I wondered why everyone except my parents loved me. I figured I wasn't really theirs. I had never gotten into fights except that one time with Jamp, after which I learned he was my brother. I hoped that my brothers and sisters were doing okay and that no one was messing with them.

School went on just fine. No one was bothering me; I thought everyone was getting along. But one day after school when we were playing flag football, a game I had never played before, I grabbed for one runner's flag and snatched and tore his shirt, which was hanging out. He got angry and looked like he wanted to fight me; he called me a nigger. We were about to engage with each other when the PE teacher blew his whistle and got between us. He blew his whistle again and had everybody come in a circle around him. He told everyone that that type of language would not be tolerated. He told us to tuck our shirts inside our pants, and he told the other PE teacher to take over the game. He led the boy to the office.

I thought I better tell Grandma that I wanted to go back home because the people there didn't want us to go to school with them. I'd been back to school for only two days and the same thing almost happened all over again. I was afraid that if I had gotten into a fight, she wouldn't have let me stay with her and that I'd have to go to Houston. Thank God that nothing happened and that I didn't have to tell her I'd almost gotten into a fight again. I hoped she would start to believe in me, and I thanked God that Steve was all right. I hoped that he'd told them what had happened and that I hadn't started that fight.

After that, it looked like things were starting to get better among the black and white students. I was on the A team for track, and my uncle was on the B team. I was really good in the fifty- and hundred-yard dashes, but our relay team wasn't very good.

One good thing happened. While I had had no family cheering me on in Louisiana, out in Vallejo, one man would always talk to me after our meets and tell me how good I was. Mr. Phil told me he had a boys' club that he wanted me to join. No one in Louisiana had taken such an interest in me. He told me that his club was at his house and that he would pick up my uncle and me at our house. I told him I'd think about it.

He was there for every track meet, and he always told me how well I was doing. He showed me a way of getting out of the blocks faster. One day, he asked me about my grades, and I told them they were good. He said that I should ask him if I ever needed help with my classes. I said, "Yes sir, I will." He laughed and asked me where I was from. Before I could answer, he said, "You must be from back South because none of the kids up here say yes sir." I said, "Yes sir, I'm from Louisiana." I didn't tell him my grades were good because I was repeating ninth grade.

One day at practice, he introduced me to some of the guys on the B and A teams who were members of his club, and they all started asking me to join his club. I asked Grandma if I could and told her about Mr. Phil. She said that she had heard of him, that he was a deacon at Friendship Baptist Church. She said, "If he'll pick y'all up and bring you home, that'll be fine."

A couple of days later at my next track meet, he asked me if I had decided to join his club. I said, "Yes sir. My grandma said it was okay."

A few days later, he picked us up, and we went to a meeting in his garage. Three or four guys were there, and five of us had driven there with him. We all knew each other. He told us his club's rules. After the first two, I knew I couldn't make the club. Number one was no smoking, and I smoked. Number two was that we had to go to church and Bible study, which I didn't do. But after I got home, I thought about how good he made me feel about myself; he was always there cheering me on. I started to stop smoking and was ready to go to church. Mr. Phil was like the father I had always wanted to be at my games. I joined the club and did my best to do all that he asked me to do.

One day, he told us that if we maintained a B average and went to church, he would pick us up and take us places, and he did exactly that. He took us places I had never been. During the basketball season, he would take us to see the Warriors play; during baseball season, he took us to see the Giants and the A's; and during football season, he took us to see the Raiders and the 49ers.

Most every Saturday, we saw college games at Stanford, Berkeley, San Francisco State, San Jose State, UC Davis, and Sacramento State. I had never seen as many people as I did at a USC-UCLA game. He took us everywhere, and we had a lot of fun. Things were looking different from the way they were in Louisiana, where I was always told where to go and not to go. Back in Louisiana, we couldn't walk on the sidewalk with a white person at the same time. We couldn't go to the same restaurants or the same schools as the white people did. I wondered about the differences, and I wondered why we didn't have segregated schools so the fighting would stop. But life with my grandmother and uncles was good.

I had been there about three months when I noticed that my uncle was treating me more like a brother than a nephew. We always went places together and had fun, and I always looked after him as I had my sisters and brothers in Louisiana. I guess we were about the same size because he would always ask to borrow my clothes, especially my jacket, and at times, he didn't even ask; I would just see him wearing it.

Whenever my grandmother gave him money, she gave me some too. I wasn't used to anyone giving me anything except TT, Dave, Par, and my uncle when he came to Louisiana from California. My parents would always ask me for the money I earned or would steal it from me.

My grandfather came home; he was a merchant seaman and was gone a lot. That was the first time I had seen him since I had gotten there. He was real nice to me, but he was also very strict. A couple of days before he came home, my grandmother had us clean the house top to bottom, and when he got home, he checked it all out to make sure everything was clean. He asked me how I was doing in school, and I told him I was doing well. He gave my uncle and me $200 each and told us to go school shopping. Man, was that different. My parents would never have done that because there were too many of us—my father didn't earn much, and my mother didn't work at all. I shook his hand and said, "Thank you, sir."

My uncle and I took the bus to Richmond to shop just as Will and I had shopped in Louisiana. On the bus, my uncle told me not to tell anyone I lived in Vallejo because people in Richmond didn't like people from Vallejo; we might get into fights over that. I started wondering again what I had gotten myself into. It seemed as if black and white students fought at school and black people fought each other in Richmond. I understood why my uncle had told me not to talk to anyone while I was waiting for them to pick me up from the bus station.

When we were shopping, it seemed as if everyone was staring at us. My uncle told me not to stare back. I don't know if I stopped that, but I didn't want to do anything to make my grandparents send me back to Louisiana. However, no one was going to intimidate me. I'd been told to never let anyone think I was afraid of them. I'd made my mind up that we might have to fight because no one was going to take my money or my clothes. I wanted to look sharp in school. I had to remind myself to control myself. Grandfather didn't take any mess off any of us. I was sure he would send me home if I got in trouble and regret they had let me come in the first place. I really enjoyed being able to go to any restaurant I wanted to. I worked at restaurants in Louisiana, but I had never been allowed to eat at any one of them.

Lorraine still told me no when I asked her out on dates. I believed she would change her mind once she'd gotten to know me better. I wouldn't have looked good to her parents if I got into fights.

I wondered about my family in Louisiana. *How's Mom's health? How's he treating her? Is he still working? Are my sisters and brothers doing okay? How do they look? How do they dress for school? Is anyone messing with them? Is my other brother still living with TT?* I wasn't there to look after them or protect them. I hoped they were looking out for each other. I wanted to get a job so I could send them money. I missed them very much. I just couldn't have lived there any longer than I had. I felt that he had never wanted me. *Why was that? What did I do? Was I a bad kid?* Nothing I had ever done had been good enough for him. I hoped one day I would make him proud and he would love me.

I thought about Jamp. I remembered times we had gone fishing. I wondered how he was doing. *Is he looking after our sisters and brothers?* I didn't have his phone number or even his address, so I couldn't even write him. I wondered if he was still with his girlfriend, Sharon. She was very pretty.

I hoped God would make Lorraine my wife, but she would just laugh when I would ask her on a date. I saw her almost every day. She was so pretty, but I thought I was just not her type. I was new there, dark skinned, and I didn't talk like they talked. They would laugh at the way I talked. She was real light skinned with long, brown hair and blue eyes. Man, she was something else. I wish Jamp could have seen her, but that wouldn't happen.

Again, I wondered if anyone would ever love me like Par, TT, Dave, and my grandparents in California did.

Psalm 94:16-18 English Standard Version (ESV)

[16] Who rises up for me against the wicked? Who stands up for me against evildoers? [17] If the LORD had not been my help, my soul would soon have lived in the land of silence.

[18] When I thought, "My foot slips," your steadfast love, O LORD, held me up.

Jeremiah 29:11 English Standard Version (ESV)

[11] For I know the plans I have for you, declares the LORD, plans for welfare[a] and not for evil, to give you a future and a hope.

How did I get here? I never heard any man call me his son? I asked myself. But I kept God first in all that I said and did, and I bless his holy name and praise him always.

I am a strong believer more than ever about the Footprints Prayer, which reminds me of perseverance and never losing faith. When I was working and walking in the fields on the plantation with God and I looked back and saw only one set of footprints, I knew he was carrying me into my future.

You persevere when you overcome your negative thoughts and don't quit before you reach your goal. Trust God. Keep Him first in all you do. He will carry you to the top. Keep that in mind if you feel someone has wronged you. Don't hold that against them or hate them; show them love because maybe they didn't know any better.

My parents were young. I don't know why they treated me the way they did, but I learned that if you hold negativity in your heart, you will never move forward. No one's perfect, but we can all never give up and achieve our goals.

Everyone knew me as Plook, my nickname. I left New Roads, Louisiana, on a Trailways bus and traveled to Richmond, California. When my uncle and grandma picked me up, they asked if I was Ernest. I said yes. That's when I stopped being Plook.

Stay tuned for the next book about my life as Ernest.

Isaiah 41:13 English Standard Version (ESV)
[13] For I, the LORD your God, hold your right hand; it is I who say to you, "Fear not, I am the one who helps you."

Matthew 6:14-15 English Standard Version (ESV)
[14] For if you forgive others their trespasses, your heavenly Father will also forgive you, [15] but if you do not forgive others their trespasses, neither will your Father forgive your trespasses.

Ephesians 6:10-18 English Standard Version (ESV)
The Whole Armor of God

[10] Finally, be strong in the Lord and in the strength of his might. [11] Put on the whole armor of God, that you may be able to stand against the schemes of the devil. [12] For we do not wrestle against flesh

and blood, but against the rulers, against the authorities, against the cosmic powers over this present darkness, against the spiritual forces of evil in the heavenly places. [13] Therefore take up the whole armor of God, that you may be able to withstand in the evil day, and having done all, to stand firm. [14] Stand therefore, having fastened on the belt of truth, and having put on the breastplate of righteousness, [15] and, as shoes for your feet, having put on the readiness given by the gospel of peace. [16] In all circumstances take up the shield of faith, with which you can extinguish all the flaming darts of the evil one; [17] and take the helmet of salvation, and the sword of the Spirit, which is the word of God, [18] praying at all times in the Spirit, with all prayer and supplication. To that end, keep alert with all perseverance, making supplication for all the saints.

Notes

Notes

Notes

Printed in the United States
By Bookmasters